Observing Children with Attachment Difficulties in School

Observing Children with Attachment Difficulties in School

A Tool for Identifying and Supporting Emotional and Social Difficulties in Children Aged 5–11

Kim S. Golding, Jane Fain, Ann Frost, Cathy Mills, Helen Worrall, Netty Roberts, Eleanor Durrant and Sian Templeton

Foreword by Louise Michelle Bombèr

Jessica Kingsley *Publishers*
London and Philadelphia

First published in 2013
by Jessica Kingsley Publishers
73 Collier Street
London N1 9BE, UK
and
400 Market Street, Suite 400
Philadelphia, PA 19106, USA

www.jkp.com

Library of Congress Cataloging in Publication Data
Golding, Kim S.
  Observing children with attachment difficulties in school : a tool for identifying and supporting
emotional and social difficulties in children aged 5-11 / Kim S. Golding, Jane Fain, Ann Frost, Cathy Mills,
Helen Worrall, Netty Roberts, Eleanor Durrant and Sian Templeton ; foreword by Louise Bomber.
       pages cm
  Includes bibliographical references.
  ISBN 978-1-84905-336-5 (alk. paper)
  1. Attachment behavior in children. 2. Children with social disabilities--Education (Elementary) 3.
Children with mental disabilities--Education (Elementary) I. Title.
  BF723.A75G654 2012
  155.42'492--dc23
                            2012039671

British Library Cataloguing in Publication Data
A CIP catalogue record for this book is available from the British Library

ISBN 978 1 84905 336 5
eISBN 978 0 85700 675 2

Printed and bound in Great Britain
by Bell and Bain Ltd, Glasgow

We dedicate the observation checklist
books to the memory of Annie Wise,
a much missed colleague and friend.

Contents

Contents

Foreword

For such a time as this …

For some time now, education staff have been increasingly concerned about a number of pupils who have not been reaching their learning potential in school. These education staff know that, despite usually good teaching practice, something is amiss.

Up until recently, access to the latest neuroscientific findings have been restricted to those involved in social services and health. Pupils who have attachment difficulties may simply have been labelled as 'attention-seeking', 'troublemakers', 'compliant', 'shy', 'problem children', or simply 'those without hope'. In homes, schools and communities alike, expectations for these children have traditionally been low and blame is often prevalent. However, all of this is changing. Education staff on the frontline working alongside many troubled pupils are beginning to understand why these pupils do what they do.

So, with increasing numbers of education staff now becoming aware of the impact of relational trauma and loss upon the capacities of pupils in their care, tools such as those recommended here are welcomed. With increased understanding, the possibilities open up and we become aware that there is much potential for adaption and recovery despite what a pupil might have experienced previously. As adults we have a shared ethical responsibility in ensuring that all children and young people are experiencing safety, security and stability – whatever our role or context. Realizing a pupil's starting point and then intervening relationally and developmentally facilitates growth, enabling the pupil to engage with his or her thinking brain. Engaging this part of the brain rather than the primal part, the brain stem – responsible for fight, flight or freeze – facilitates opportunity, exploration, learning and achievement. This book provides clear descriptors of some of the possible vulnerabilities around for these pupils and a framework through which to make sense of these vulnerabilities with an attachment focus.

What is going on at home, what has happened in the past, and the impact of the 'here and now' in school is often viewed as a mere excuse for behaviours. Here we have a clear framework whereby we can make sense of behaviours. These pupils don't need our scorn or pity, but someone in school to take account of their stories so that they can then have access to the most appropriate types of support. Time is precious.

It is not complicated. If we engage in more reflective practice using this framework, we are then in a position to make a difference. The impact of relational trauma and loss need not be a life sentence. At this time we have become overly concerned with diagnoses when what these pupils really need is our time, patience and sensitive care in view of where they are at. They need us. When did we start thinking that only experts could make a difference? Relationships in school are much more powerful than we realize. Never before have we been given such evidence and permission to engage in quality relationships with these pupils so that they can thrive. Facilitating a secure base for pupils in school is essential in order for their exploratory system to come online. We don't need to wait. There is so much we can do now, integrating this approach into everyday school life. This book can only increase our curiosity about pupils – as we wonder why they do what they do. This curiosity is essential in support work. The checklist provides a window into the way pupils view themselves, others, and the contexts they find themselves in. This window will give us all the clues we need for introducing helpful interventions in school.

At this time when resources are limited and finance restricted, we need tools that will not only skill ourselves up further as education staff, but also flag up those with more severe need so that these pupils aren't left floundering when their brains are growing most optimally. I like the way this book clearly presents many of the issues that need addressing, meaning that we are more likely to ensure limited resources are matched more appropriately, so that we are cost effective in the approaches used. It is clear that many of our current approaches with vulnerable pupils are not working – as evidenced by the increased use of detentions and exclusions – and so it is time for a rethink.

The detail found later on in the book is particularly helpful for those who already have a basic understanding of attachment and want to explore these matters in greater depth. The explanations are succinct and so helpful in raising awareness of these pupils' needs and in advocating for what they most need within our schools in order to 'settle to learn'.

Throughout the book there are short case studies used to support understanding, and they do. On page upon page we are introduced to the world of attachment. To date teacher training has not included much psychology and we realize now that it should have done. Organizations such as the Nurture Group Network (www.nurturegroups.org) have been advocating for these pupils and encouraging relational and developmental support in schools since the 1960s. The findings of Bowlby, Winnicott, Schore, Stern, Levine, Howe, Fonagy, Hughes, Porges and Perry have still not been integrated into mainstream education policy and practice yet – why?

Those on the frontline need access to further reading and training based on the research of those involved in developmental trauma and loss. Dr Golding and her colleagues have made a significant contribution to inclusive practice by writing this book. I'm sure you will find many examples contained here that will gently challenge assumptions made over the years. For example, we have attempted to teach emotional literacy without realizing that for some pupils who have not had someone physically present, attentive, attuned and responsive to their needs that experience comes first. Experience comes before understanding.

Much of what these pupils need to learn can't be learnt alone through textbooks. They need you and me. Relationships matter. In school let's take up our responsibility in ensuring that these pupils experience healthy secure attachment in our care so that they can be all that they can and want to be, making valuable contributions towards our shared society.

For such a time as this …

Louise Michelle Bombèr
June 2012

Acknowledgements

Our first acknowledgement is for Annie Wise. Annie was an education psychologist, who provided support to the Integrated Service for Looked After Children (ISL). The vision for an observation checklist first came about following some initial discussions between Jane Fain and Annie. They began to discuss the need for ISL to have something that would help them to reflect on children's behaviours, and the emotional needs these revealed. They wanted to help early years practitioners and teachers deepen their understanding of the children in their care. Sadly Annie died before this vision could be realized, but Jane kept the idea alive. It is a testament to Annie's enthusiasm that this checklist is now an essential part of the ISL toolkit. We thank Annie for paving the way, enabling us to continue in her footsteps.

Worcestershire schools are very fortunate in having an additional service that has an emphasis on supporting looked after and adopted children. ISL practitioners are able to support schools in staying curious and reflective about a child's behaviour. The ISL education support teams (teams one and three) understand that meeting emotional needs is an important prerequisite to meeting the social and then the learning needs of a child. ISL teachers, classroom practitioners, mentors and child support workers make sure that this message is heard within schools. The community and leisure team extends this support from school to community, while the work of team two helps school and home to be joined up.

A number of people have provided advice to us during the development of this tool. Our thanks go to the schools who agreed to pilot the tool in its initial stages. Thanks also to Hannah Careme for advice about sensory integration needs, and all our colleagues within the three teams of ISL, who have been generous with their support and ideas.

Demands of day-to-day working and heavy workloads can make it difficult to set time aside for creative and innovative development. This time would not be found without the support of managers who believe in the vision and agree the development time. We would therefore like to thank managers past and present for their enduring support: team managers and senior social workers Helen, Liz, Ellie, Kathy, Claire, Wendy, Lisa, Vicki and Karol; operational managers Julie, Ann and Wendy (again); service managers Julie (again) and in Worcestershire Child and Adolescent Mental Health Services (CAMHS) Jenni, Su and Fran.

Thanks to Steve, and everyone at JKP who have helped produce this book and the companion book for preschool settings.

Finally our thanks go to Louise Michelle Bombèr, who has been a source of encouragement, giving us the confidence to publish our work.

Introduction

This resource has been designed to assist those working in schools to recognize the emotional needs of the children and the difficulties they may have in benefiting from the support on offer.

It is intended to be used as a tool to reflect on the child's behaviour and, using attachment theory as a guide, consider what this may be communicating and how this can be supported. The observation checklist which forms the heart of the resource is designed to help structure observations of children in school – to identify their support needs – and will be especially helpful in understanding the child with attachment insecurities or difficulties.

With the information acquired through structured observations, staff will be better equipped to find creative ways of meeting the relationship needs of the children, building emotional health where there is emotional difficulty and equipping children for a continuing journey through education within which they will be able to benefit relationally, emotionally, socially and then educationally.

We will first provide readers with accessible summaries of the information and background theory they need in order to understand the developmental challenges and difficulties that these children face, before providing more information about the checklist and how it can be used in Chapters 4 to 8.

We then provide guidance on how to help support the children in the classroom.

Before reading on, you may prefer to take a quick look at the checklist itself in Appendix 1 to get a sense of what it looks like and the form it takes.

The material in this checklist is universal, and applicable for professionals working with school children in any country, even though terminology (such as Key Stage 1 and 2/primary school; nursery/kindergarden) differs. As this observation checklist was developed and piloted in Worcestershire, England, we use UK terminology throughout, but include a short glossary in Appendix 4 which explains specific UK terminology.

Many chapters contain useful summaries; these are marked with ⬦ and readers have permission to download them for their personal use from www.jkp.com/catalogue/book/9781849053365/resources.

1 Child Development in the Early Years

The human infant, beyond any other species, is born immature and dependent. This is partly a consequence of our evolutionary development. As our species developed, our brain size increased and therefore our heads became larger compared to other mammals. If we were born with fully mature brains babies would need larger heads making it impossible for them to pass through the birth canal. For this reason babies are born with immature brains and relatively small heads. This means that much of brain development needs to occur postnatally. This result of human development works very well for us as a social species, pushing brain development as it does into the social world. We are a product of how we are cared for (for an accessible text exploring this, see Gerhardt 2004).

Here are a few facts to support the importance of early experience and how it impacts on children coming into education and how they relate to others (see Gerhardt 2004; Nash 1997).

- A human infant's brain almost doubles in size during the first year.

- At birth the baby has all the brain cells (neurons) it needs in place, but these cells are immature. At birth the neurons are mostly unconnected, but by three years of age there is a dense network of connections.

- Genes begin the process of brain development, but it is experience that triggers the electrical activity which will determine how the neurons connect and grow.

- The development of the brain is therefore experience-dependent. It develops as a consequence of experience and through interactions with others.

- Between birth and the age of two, there is a critical period for emotional growth that supports cognitive development, thinking and growth.

- If the child lives in fear, the brain chemistry changes. This means that children come into settings with an altered or distorted way of thinking and processing information.

Human babies are well equipped for development within a social world, being attracted to other people and equipped to seek nurture and care from those around them. They instinctively elicit from others what they need to nourish the brain. This also gives them their greatest vulnerability. If the social world is not able to give the babies what they need, brain development will suffer. When children's early dependency needs are not met, this can have a lifelong impact, not only on emotional and social development but also on learning. A critical factor in whether children recover from this earliest of traumas is the quality of the later relationships they encounter throughout their childhood. Many of these relationships will be in educational settings.

An early sign of emotional difficulty is displayed through the development of first attachment relationships. Children who are not able to receive sensitive, responsive, nurturing care for a variety of reasons will develop attachment relationships adapted to this lack. Described as attachment insecurities or, for the most severely affected, attachment difficulties, these are adaptations to a world which is not meeting the most fundamental of emotional needs, to be kept safe and secure. This can impact on the child's journey into the wider world outside of the home.

Children may not get their attachment needs met for a variety of reasons. Illness and/or hospitalization in child or parent, neurodevelopmental difficulty in child or parent or experience of separation, loss, abuse and neglect for the child can all be factors in the development of attachment difficulties. This leaves these children disadvantaged at the very beginning of their life. The secure base of home is missing and they adapt to a world without it. The cost is a slowed or disordered emotional development, and an emotional immaturity which will have later impact on the rest of development. This leaves the child at risk for a range of emotional, social and cognitive difficulties. Most importantly the ability to form and benefit from relationships is compromised. In adapting to the lack of relationship in their early life, the children are affected in the area that could also provide them with greatest healing. Parents and other significant adults who want to help these children are ready to offer relationships to the children. The children, however, have not learnt how to use and benefit from such relationships because of the lack of experience in their earliest months or years. To help these children, we cannot just offer them relationships; we also need to help them to use and benefit from these relationships.

As the children continue along their life's journey, their horizons will widen to also include the world of education. Children enter school according to their chronological age and not dependent upon the stage of development that they are at. Some are ready for this step into the wider world while others are not. School staff are prepared for these differences and will provide individualized support. The biggest challenge facing them, however, is how to meet the needs of the children who have not had their earliest dependency needs met and are therefore least ready for the relative independence of school. Louise Michelle Bombèr tells us:

> We cannot fast-track children who have experienced trauma and loss into emotional and sensory literacy, without first giving them the opportunity to fully negotiate the developmental stage of dependency. Self and other awareness grows in the context of a positive, sensitive and caring relationship, in which the child is initially dependent on an adult: this relationship is what we must provide in schools. (Bombèr 2007, p.10)

If children are to be successful social beings, if they are to be successful learners and if they are to be emotionally healthy enough to have relationship success, it is imperative that those working in schools are equipped to recognize and meet the emotional needs of the children in their care. For children with attachment difficulties, these needs can be presented in a range of ways, not all of which are obvious, and the children can have a range of challenges in being able to use the support and nurture being offered.

2 Recognizing the Emotional Needs of Children in School

This chapter features scenarios to illustrate the different emotional needs of a number of different school children.

Amanda, John and Niko are walking to school. It is the beginning of the week and they are all clutching something in their hands.

Amanda strides out confidently, a little ahead of her mother. She looks eager to arrive. As they approach the playground, she runs up to the gate. She gives a little look back to her mother, who gives a slight nod, and then runs in. By the time Mum catches up with her, she is already getting into line, chatting to the girl ahead of her. Her school bag has been dropped beside her. Mum picks it up and gently hands it back to Amanda. She reminds her to place it on her peg as soon as the teacher lets them in. Mum steps back and watches the teacher come out and organize the children. Amanda looks over to her mum and gives her a smile. Mum gives a quick wave and then watches as she walks into the classroom, bag in hand.

John appears less confident. He walks with his father, who chats to him about the day ahead and what he is going to do. They walk across the playground together and Dad guides him into his line. John does not want to take his place until he is sure that Dad is going to stand and watch him go in to school. Dad shows him where he is going to stand and, settled now, John gives Dad a hug. He watches Dad as he moves to the side of the playground. The teacher comes out to organize the children. John looks over to Dad anxiously, making sure that he is still there. Dad gives a wave and watches as John walks into the classroom still looking over at him.

Niko is the most reluctant of these three children. He holds on to his mother's hand, almost holding back as they walk up the road. When they reach the playground he falters, not wanting to go in. Mum bends down and encourages him on, giving him a light hug to reassure him that she will support him. Slowly they move across to the gate. Niko makes no attempt to go in or to join the line. Mum accepts this and stays with him while he gathers up his courage to move on. A teaching assistant comes up to support Niko. She encourages Mum and Niko to follow her to the line where Mum leaves him with her as they have agreed. Niko cries as she goes, but allows himself to be comforted by the teaching assistant, who keeps him close to her.

These children will be familiar to anyone working in primary school. They represent the range of individual differences that children can display. Some children are sociable, confident and bubbly; others are more reserved, while others are shy and uncomfortable. Children of the same age vary in maturity and the degree to which they demonstrate temperamental traits, such as sociability and shyness. Some children take everything in their stride, thriving on the unexpected, while others are slower to warm up, preferring predictability and consistency. This represents the individual differences within the emotional and social development of young children. The sensitive teacher adapts his or her approach to each of the children depending upon their needs, and each child is able to grow in confidence and security as the school year progresses. They remain different from each other, but each child is able to benifit from the experience of school. Children have individual differences but with appropriate support will make progress in their social and emotional development. This in turn allows them to benefit from everything the school has to offer and thus to progress in their learning.

What makes these children different from those we would describe as having an emotional difficulty? These are children who will require more specialized help from the teachers and assistants in the school. In many ways recognizing children with emotional difficulties can be difficult precisely because children show a range of individual differences.

Amanda is sociable and confident. How can we distinguish her from Karen, who also comes in confidently in the morning? Karen, however, is a little overly boisterous. Other children warm to Amanda but appear more wary of Karen, who can be controlling and domineering. When it is time for assembly, Amanda and Karen are keen to go in. Amanda walks into the hall, seeking out her friends to sit with, while being aware of where her teacher is. Karen rushes into the hall, pushing herself among the children. She takes no notice of the teacher as she demands that the child next to her move up a little.

John is quieter and more reserved. Jack also appears quiet and reserved, but when the boys are observed together, there is a confidence in John that is not apparent in Jack. John will get on with the task in front of him, but as the adult approaches he is able to accept support and to go further in what he is doing as a result. He tends to gravitate to one or two of the other children, but is not overly concerned when paired up with a different child. Jack is less easy to support, and progresses less well under the adult's careful gaze. He finds it harder to adjust to children outside of his small group. When it is time for assembly, both boys will respond to the teacher's instruction and move on into the hall. Jack, however, will appear more on edge during the assembly. He complies, with the teacher's encouragement, but is less comfortable doing so.

Niko is shy and quiet. He needs extra support to cope with daily routines and to cope with change and transition. George also appears shy, but is much more clingy and needy of support. Neither Niko nor George cope well with assembly. Niko can cope as long as he is supported by a familiar adult, whereas George is more likely to go to pieces, clinging to the adult until the assembly is over. Throughout the year it is Amanda, John and Niko who make most progress, while Karen, Jack and George remain of concern to those supporting them.

Differentiating between children who are different but emotionally reasonably secure within these differences and those who are more emotionally troubled can be a difficult task. The teachers and assistants need to be aware of a range of information in order to be able to pick out the children who will need additional and carefully tailored support.

- First, the child's behaviour in school is clearly important. Getting to know each child and how he or she copes with different situations and activities provides a wealth of knowledge that can help to identify the children in most trouble emotionally.

- Second, the progress the child is making will also provide important information concerning what additional support a child might need. Children making good social, emotional and learning progress are clearly benefiting from what they are being offered. Where progress is slow, it may be that the child needs something different in the support he or she is receiving.

The observation checklist can assist in both of these areas, guiding the worker in observing the behaviours that the child is displaying and offering a way of monitoring the changes or lack of change in these behaviours over time.

There is a third area of information that is also important to take into account and can help in interpreting the observations being made with the help of the checklist:

- The contextual information provided by knowledge of the child's early and current experience. What has happened and is happening at home? Are there home difficulties that have always been present, or is there some more immediate stress that the child has to deal with?

Children who are encountering current stress will need additional support in the school. If this stress is temporary and with good home–school communication, the child is likely to be relatively easily supported, and will continue to make progress over the year. Where there have been past difficulties that have impacted on emotional development and well-being, and especially when these difficulties are ongoing, the child may need more tailored and ongoing support in the school and progress is likely to be slower. These are the children, whose attachment development may have been compromised, making it harder for them to use the support of the staff and assistants in the school. For example:

- Children may have had early illnesses compromising the development of security at home. This can include children who have a challenging birth history, prematurity, or other reasons for spending time in a special care baby unit, delaying their arrival home. Any hospitalization during the early years can compromise the development of security with caregivers, thus leading to difficulties in attachment.

- Children may have experienced illness in a parent. A parent may have been hospitalized, or may be suffering from an illness that makes it more difficult to be available and responsive to his or her young child. Postnatal depression is an obvious example of such an illness.

- Stress within the family that is overwhelming to the parent or parents can also lead to insecurity for the child. Any stress, such as unemployment, poverty or family strife, which makes the parent less responsive or available to the child is likely to impact on the child's attachment security and emotional development.

- Children born with a learning difficulty may find it harder to express their needs to their parent. These parents may therefore struggle to identify these needs and thus to help the child to feel secure.

- Parents who have their own early history of trauma and/or compromised parenting are likely to find it harder to be available and responsive to the child.

- Parents who are actively neglectful or abusive to the child, or whose lifestyle is impacting negatively on their parenting. Substance abuse, domestic violence, instability, changes of partner, utilization of a range of caregivers to look after the child are all experiences that are likely to be traumatizing for the child, sitting alongside physical abuse, sexual abuse and emotional abuse and neglect as experiences that have the most detrimental impact on attachment formation and emotional development.

- Children living in foster care, adopted or living with family on a residence or special guardianship order. While these children are not necessarily emotionally distressed by their early experience, they have all had experience of separation and loss of birth family. A significant proportion of these children will also have experienced early traumatic care. These children are therefore at increased risk of a range of emotional difficulties.

Understanding the development of attachments and how this impacts on the emotional development of the child is therefore important underpinning knowledge for supporting the child with social and emotional difficulties in school.

Chapter 3 provides a summary of attachment theory and how understanding this theory can inform how we help to support children.

3 Understanding Emotional Needs through Knowledge of Attachment Theory

In this chapter attachment theory is briefly summarized, and this working knowledge should be sufficient for the reader wanting to use the checklist. However, for those interested in a more detailed account, we provide an extended explanation in Appendix 2.

Attachment theory has been developed over many decades and is based on the pioneering work of John Bowlby (Bowlby 1973, 1980, 1982, 1998). It is a theory about the special form of affectional bond that develops between a child and a parent within which the child experiences security and comfort from the parent.

Attachment theory is therefore a theory about first relationships, and how these relationships impact on a child's journey through life. Early attachment experience influences the way children develop later relationships and how they learn to rely on others for help and support. This in turn influences the way that children develop belief and a sense of efficacy in themselves, and how they learn to rely on others. A secure attachment therefore promotes both dependence (the ability to use others for support) and independence (the ability to rely on self).

To start at the beginning, when children are born, they need a 'primary carer' (attachment figure) to help them feel safe and secure. If the primary carer is temporarily not there, a few familiar adults can substitute for this carer (secondary attachment figures). When children derive some security from their attachment figures, they feel safe enough to explore and play in the world. Children can experience worry, fear or need for comfort for a range of reasons. When something new or unknown is happening, when they are feeling tired or unwell or when the children experience or anticipate that parents are not available when they need them.

If young children start to feel worry, fear or need for comfort, it is important that they have close contact with someone with whom they have developed an attachment. They need close physical contact with this person to soothe them when upset. As they get older, this can be verbal instead of physical contact, although if they are sufficiently stressed, physical contact will still be preferred.

Patterns of attachment

Patterns of attachment develop in relation to the way that attachment figures respond to the child:

- When he or she has attachment needs stemming from the experience of worry, fear or a need for comfort.

- When he or she is looking for support for exploration and play.

This will affect the child's capacity to develop relationships and ability to manage feelings as he or she grows, develops and matures.

Descriptions of attachment patterns do vary among researchers into attachment theory. In this book we use the more traditional A B C + D model of attachment patterns, which sets out four distinct attachment styles relating to the early experience of the children. This contrasts with the alternative Dynamic Maturational Model (DMM) developed by Patricia Crittenden (Crittenden 2008; Crittenden, Landini and Claussen 2001). In the DMM, attachment patterns are described as developing dynamically as the child matures, with increasingly controlling behaviours emerging when the child experiences a continuing lack of safety. Both models emphasize organization of behaviour in order to achieve feelings of safety, with the development of highly controlling behaviours to manage relationships that feel dangerous. The reader who would like to explore these differing models is referred to Howe (2011).

Secure attachment pattern (B)

When a parent is available to meet the need for comfort as displayed by the child, and can support the child in play and exploration, a secure attachment will develop. Children with a secure attachment pattern appear confident. Whether quiet or lively, these children will appear to relish the challenges that life offers. They are confident to have a go, but will also seek help when needed.

Insecure patterns

Insecure avoidant pattern (A)

An insecure avoidant pattern of attachment develops out of a relationship with a carer who is distant and rejecting. The carer finds it difficult to cope with the child's emotional needs. These children start to worry when they experience strong feelings in themselves or others. They are often keen to please and to do things right. When these children do feel angry, often their anger appears to suddenly erupt. These children can mask negative feelings with false positive affect – the child who smiles whether feeling happy or sad (e.g. see Crittenden 2008).

Children with insecure avoidant patterns can appear withdrawn and quiet or more self-reliant than expected for their age. They are more focused on 'doing' than people.

They do not like to be dependent upon others and are therefore less likely to turn to adults to seek help.

Insecure ambivalent pattern (C)

An insecure ambivalent pattern of attachment develops out of a relationship with a carer who will sometimes meet the child's needs, but this is more dependent on his or her mood than the child's need.

Children with insecure ambivalent attachment patterns can appear attention-needing, and find it difficult to settle by themselves or with groups of children. They will sometimes talk excessively, or act as a 'clown' in order to keep adult attention. They find it difficult to concentrate on activities as they are concentrating on their need for adult attention.

Disorganized/disorientated and controlling attachment pattern (D)

The disorganized/disorientated and controlling attachment pattern develops out of a relationship within which the parent is frightened of or frightening to the child. Parents can be frightened parenting a child if they had experienced being frightened when they themselves were parented. They become very unavailable and unresponsive to the child when that child is in most need of their presence and support. This is as frightening to a child as parents who are overtly frightening because they shout, punish the child, expose the child to family violence or behave oddly because of substance abuse or mental illness.

These are the children who have the hardest time feeling safe. When they feel scared, children turn to their parent or attachment figure to reduce this fear. The parent is a source of comfort. When the parent is both the potential source of comfort and also the biggest threat to them, the children are faced with a dilemma – I need you, but you are frightening me. Infants and toddlers appear disorientated and struggle to organize their behaviour in a way which helps them to feel safe in the face of this threat.

As they grow beyond toddlerhood, these children solve the problem of having a carer who is a source both of comfort and of fear by taking control of relationships. Thus their behaviour appears more organized. They become very controlling in all their relationships, developing self-reliant or coercive ways of relating with others. Some of these children appear hyper-alert, aggressive and challenging. Others appear more 'switched off' and unresponsive.

How children bring attachment difficulties into school

Children use their early attachment experience to build up a sort of template of how relationships work. This is called an 'internal working model'. This template guides them in what to expect from others and what to believe about themselves. For example, secure children will believe that they are likeable to others and that others will be available to support them. Insecure children will doubt their 'likeability' and will anticipate that others are less likely to be available to them.

When children move away from the home, they will engage in relationships outside of their family. Children will approach these new relationships based on their previous experience. We anticipate in the future what we have known in the past. A secure child will expect to be liked and that others will support him or her. An insecure child will not have this confidence.

Let us return to the examples of the children we introduced in Chapter 2. Amanda, John and Niko all experienced security of attachment. While they all approached school differently, they were all able to use their parent to support them to make the transition to school. They could all transfer this 'secure base' to the teacher or teaching assistant, and thus gain support to manage the day away from the parent. Karen, Jack and George do not have this attachment security. They are much less able to draw security from their parents. The transition to school is therefore more challenging, and they are less able either to seek support from the teacher or teaching assistant or to use this support when they have got it. This inability to use emotional support will impact not only on their feelings of security or safety while at school, but also on their emotional development. They will remain emotionally immature, making slower progress in their emotional development. This in turn affects their social development. They will feel less in tune with the other children and it will be harder for them to form and maintain friendships. It will also impact on their ability to learn. When we do not feel secure we become preoccupied with the need for safety, and this makes it much harder to face outwards to the world, to enjoy challenges, and to learn and develop new skills.

Amanda, John and Niko will benefit from their school experience. Karen, Jack and George will need some additional support to do so. Recognizing the Karens, Jacks and Georges is therefore an important task for those working in schools. Observing these children, monitoring their progress in emotional and social development, and being aware of their current and past experience will all be important. This information will help the teachers and teaching assistants to support the children to enjoy and benefit from the substantial amount of time they spend in school. This will in turn impact on their social and emotional development both now and in the future, providing them with the best foundation for their learning.

4 Introducing the Observation Checklist

We all need to feel safe and emotionally secure in our everyday environments. Nowhere is this more important than for a child having experience of an educational setting. Research shows that in order for children to begin to develop their academic skills, they first need to have experienced positive early attachments. These relationships are needed before their 'learning behaviours' can begin to develop (Pianta 2006). Meeting the emotional needs of children in school is therefore a priority and must precede meeting their academic needs. The observation checklist has been designed as a tool to help education practitioners with this endeavour. In this chapter the checklist is introduced alongside general guidance for using this tool.

Purpose of the checklist

As explained in the introduction to this book, this observation checklist has been designed to help to structure observations of children in school, with the aim of better understanding the needs of the children. In particular, the checklist focuses the observer on the attachment, emotional and social behaviours being displayed. Interpretation of these observations can then lead to a greater understanding of the needs of the child in these areas. It is anticipated that this tool will be especially helpful in understanding the child with attachment insecurities or difficulties.

While this checklist can be used to increase understanding of a child, and the child's emotional needs, this is *not* a diagnostic tool. Therefore, it is important not to make a diagnosis or label a child as having a specific difficulty on the basis of these observations.

As you read through the guidance below, you may find it helpful to refer to the checklist itself, which can be found in Appendix 1. Ensure also that this chapter and Chapter 5 are referred to as the checklist is completed, because these give important guidance and prompt questions that help further reflect on how a child presents in school.

When to use the checklist

The observation checklist is useful to identify the social and emotional difficulties that a child is encountering, and to monitor the child's progress over time. It will give teachers and teaching assistants some clear targets to work towards.

This checklist is designed for children at Key Stages 1 and 2. These children are aged between six and eleven years.

There are a range of situations which might prompt the use of the checklist:

- Practitioners may be concerned about behaviours being displayed by a child, especially when these behaviours are challenging and disruptive. In order to successfully manage these behaviours, while also building security for the child, it is important to understand how the behaviours reflect the internal experience of the child. The checklist will help you to focus on the emotional needs of the child and to better understand the behavioural messages being communicated. This reflection about a child's behaviours and emotional needs helps the observer to look more closely at why a child may be presenting in a particular way and helps them to view each child with the curiosity and empathy that is so important when planning support.

- The astute practitioner will also be concerned about the child who is not overtly displaying disruptive behaviours, but is in emotional difficulty nevertheless. These children don't cause trouble because they prefer to be 'invisible'. They rarely or never ask for help and appear very independent; they can also appear aloof or isolated from the other children. The only indications that they are having difficulty may be that they are socially inept or immature. Often these factors are not linked to their emotional needs and these children are 'missed' because their behaviours are not causing disruption in the setting. Additionally, their independence misleads the staff into thinking that they are coping as they should. After all, isn't that what the Early Years Foundation Stage (EYFS) and school are designed to encourage: independent, confident, self-motivated, free-thinking children? The observation checklist can help staff to rethink their opinion of this type of behaviour; to notice that the child's emotional needs are overtaking his or her ability to make the academic progress needed to reach his or her potential.

- The observation checklist can also be a really useful reflective tool even if there are no particular problems identified; it acts as a vehicle for raising awareness of the child's needs, and of demonstrating the success of current strategies being used with the child.

- Staff can also use the checklist as a tool to monitor the child through a period of change or transition, for example, when a child is moving school or class, or perhaps because of a change in his or her home situation. In this situation it can be helpful to have a checklist completed at a time when the child is settled in a familiar setting and is being appropriately supported. If necessary previous successful strategies can be implemented again and the checklist used to monitor if these are helping once again.

It is worth reiterating that the observation checklist is not a formal assessment and should not be used as a diagnostic tool. It is useful in understanding a child's emotional needs. The profile that is built up from the observations and contextual information can be used to help the practitioners consider a child's behaviour, presentation and underlying experience and to reflect on the child's attachment style shown in the school. A child may present very differently in different settings and at different times and this checklist can be useful in guiding strategies and interventions to support a child.

Making observations and recording on the checklist

Figure 4.1 summarizes how to use the observation checklist.

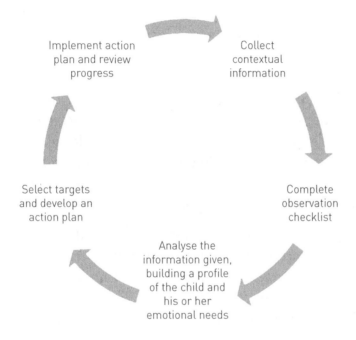

FIGURE 4.1 USING THE OBSERVATION CHECKLIST

Who can complete the checklist?

It is recommended that the checklist is completed by a person familiar with the child. If the child is relatively new to the school, the checklist can be completed by the person who is spending most time getting to know the child.

Generally where the observer is already familiar with the child, the checklist can be completed over a few days. With less familiarity, it is more likely that the checklist will be completed over a few weeks. This is a guide only; practitioners will find that the time needed will vary from child to child, and in line with the complexity of difficulties that the child presents.

In a nursery or early years setting within the UK, children are assigned a key person. This individual has responsibility to work with a small number of children, helping the children to feel safe and cared for. The key person will develop relationships with the children and their families. This key person is therefore an ideal person to complete a checklist for an individual child. At Key Stages 1 and 2 there is currently no requirement to assign a key person, but most primary school classrooms have a learning support assistant or teaching assistant and therefore they are in a good position to take up this role. Identifying a person to build a relationship with the child will be important, however; this familiarity will provide a basis for completing the checklist. The key person model is a useful one for supporting the use of the observation checklist.

How can observations be made?

The checklist provides the observer with a tool to aid observation and reflection about an individual child. This increases understanding about the child and his or her emotional and social needs. The checklist is completed based upon the observer's routine observations of the child together with his or her knowledge of the child. This can be supplemented by more structured observation if this is helpful. The observer might, for example, reflect upon a typical day for the child, and then supplement this with structured observations to gain further information. One teacher, for example, found it helpful to structure some observations of the child in different situations. She observed the child when there was a stranger in the room, while doing a familiar task and while doing a task that was more challenging. These observations were then integrated into the ongoing observations that were happening anyway as part of the classroom routine.

There is no right or wrong way of doing this; some of the checklist will be completed based on prior experience with the child, while other parts might be completed based on a new observation. In this way a profile is built up about the child guided by the sections of the checklist. This therefore is not a snapshot but a best fit between the observations made and the information on the checklist based on ongoing observation and knowledge of the child.

Within school practitioners are making observations of the children on an ongoing basis. This checklist is not intended to add to this workload, but rather to guide the observer. The checklist will be completed based both on observations that are already being made during day-to-day interactions and by focusing the observations in a different way. In this way the checklist guides the observer to reflect on behaviours in a new way and to notice behaviours that might otherwise go unnoticed.

These observations can then be supplemented by the observer standing back and watching the child. For example, the observer may not have had an opportunity to notice how the child behaves while separating from the parent or carer at the beginning of the day. He or she may therefore choose to watch the child entering the school for a few days so that this part of the checklist can be completed.

It can be helpful to discuss observations of the child with others. This provides multiple perspectives about the child which can enrich the information being gathered. For example, a teaching assistant might discuss his or her observations with the teacher.

Recording observations on the checklist

Here we provide general guidance for recording observations. More detailed, section-by-section guidance can be found in Chapter 5. The observations are recorded on the checklist by ticking the box or boxes which most closely resemble the child. This can be done gradually over days or weeks, thus building up a profile of the child. The observation period, as listed on the front of the checklist, is therefore not a set period of time. The observer can use this section to make a note of when the checklist was completed.

There are also opportunities on the checklist to record examples of the behaviours observed, and to make notes about the observations. If the observer is unsure about how to complete a section, a further few days of observation might be helpful, with this section particularly in mind.

Some children will demonstrate different behaviours at different times, sometimes demonstrating behaviours on both ends of the checklist. These differences can be recorded by ticking more than one box in a particular row of the checklist. Again the comments section can be used to record notes about these different behaviours, perhaps noting various situations within which differing behaviours were noticed. For example, while watching a child interact with other children, the observer might notice that he or she is controlling and bossy with some children but is more easily led by others. This child would get a tick at either end of the row, with a comment added about the observation, noting any differences in the children who elicit this contrasting response. 'X is bossy with children who are emotionally younger or more passive but is more easily led by the more mature or more confident children in the group.'

Using the checklist to monitor progress over time

It can be helpful to revisit the checklist after an interval of time in order to monitor what progress the child is making, or to see if the child's behaviour changes when circumstances change. For example, a checklist might have been completed for a child and then some time later the child's home circumstances change, perhaps parents separate or the child moves placement. Repeating the observations can help the practitioners to see how these changes are impacting on the child in school. Alternatively the checklist might be revisited when a child moves to a new group or class, to monitor how the child is coping with the change. In some schools practitioners might want to use the checklist at the beginning of the year so that they have a record of observations that can be used as a comparison as the child progresses through the year.

When repeating observations, the same checklist can be used for an individual child to aid easy comparison, with different colour ink being used to distinguish between the observation periods.

Supplementing the observation with contextual information

Contextual information can supplement and inform the understanding gained by the observations made with the guidance of the checklist. Here are some examples:

- Alongside using the checklist to observe the child within school, it is useful to have some discussions with the child's parents or current carers regarding the child's background, early life experiences, and the child's current functioning at home. If the child has a social worker, he or she can also be a useful source of information.

- Understanding the cultural background of the child will aid interpretation of the observations. The behaviours need to be understood against the background of any cultural differences demonstrated by the child. For example, imagine a Japanese child in a western classroom; it is likely that this child will be a bit more self-contained and quiet compared to a western child. This child might also demonstrate less eye-contact. If culture is not taken into account, the child might be recorded as difficult to relate to by familiar adults in the attachment section, and might be seen as overly timid when observing play behaviours. These behaviours are in fact culturally typical rather than being a sign of emotional or social insecurity.

- Understanding any learning difficulties displayed by the child. A child with generalized learning difficulty might, for example, be at a different stage of play or social development, explaining some of the differences the child displays when compared to peers. For example, a child might be reluctant to engage in new play or tasks. The observer needs to consider whether this reluctance is an indication of emotional insecurity or whether the task is too advanced for the child given his or her level of learning difficulty.

- An understanding about the impact of poor parenting upon children will be useful background information with which to approach understanding an individual child more deeply. In particular, understanding the attachment needs that these children may have due to their early life experiences can provide a context for this understanding. This information can help with the shift in thinking from a focus on behaviour to considering the child's emotional state.

With this awareness and background understanding, the observer can approach the completion of the checklist confidently allowing a deepening understanding of the emotional and social needs highlighted.

5

Detailed Guidance for Completing the Checklist Section by Section

In this chapter we discuss the different sections that feature within the checklist and their significance. For each section of the checklist we provide information about why we have included it, followed by guidance for making the observations. We have also included illustrations for each section which provide a quick guide to help with recording observations on the checklist. These indicate the sorts of behaviours you might observe related to each side of the checklist. Whether you rate these behaviours as 'sometimes' or 'almost always' will depend upon the frequency or intensity with which these behaviours are displayed.

Behaviour

Attachment and emotional difficulties are generally displayed through behaviour (see Section 1 of checklist). Understanding behaviour in terms of underlying emotion is therefore an important part of the observation of the child.

What is child's behaviour like?

Think about the behaviour that the child is generally displaying, and how this compares to a typical child of this age. Be aware of the 'too good' child as well as the overtly challenging child, as he or she may need additional support that hasn't been recognized.

Attention, concentration and activity levels?

Children who have had difficulties early in life often demonstrate developmental delays in ability to attend, concentrate and regulate impulses (be able to think before acting). These children may need extra support, with particular attention to the environment and how it can support these developments. Children who are overly controlled in terms of their self management of behaviour and emotions can also be struggling, although for these children it may be less obvious.

Questions to consider

- Does the child have difficulty regulating high arousal? Children who when they get excited or agitated find it hard to calm themselves down have poor emotional regulation. Children who are unpredictable, challenging and struggling with boundaries may be hyper-aroused. They may need an adult to co-regulate increasing arousal, that is, to stay with them and to help them calm down.

- Does the child have difficulty regulating low arousal? Children who are hypo-aroused (low arousal levels) may be equally in need of co-regulation by an adult.

- Does the child have difficulty with poor concentration, attention, high activity and/or impulse control? Often these children need supervision and structure suitable for a younger child, with attention to reducing the stimulation in the environment.

- Does the child appear overly controlled and/or inactive? Less obviously these children too may be struggling with the demands of the environment, but are trying to deal with this themselves rather than turning to adults for help.

What is child's behaviour like?

This illustration provides guidance on observations you might make in relation to the child's behaviour that might suggest he or she should be rated towards one side or the other on the checklist.

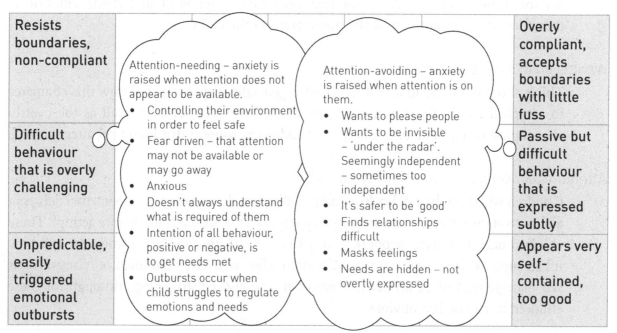

Attention, concentration and activity levels?

This illustration provides guidance on observations you might make in relation to the child's attention, concentration and activity levels that might suggest he or she should be rated towards one side or the other on the checklist.

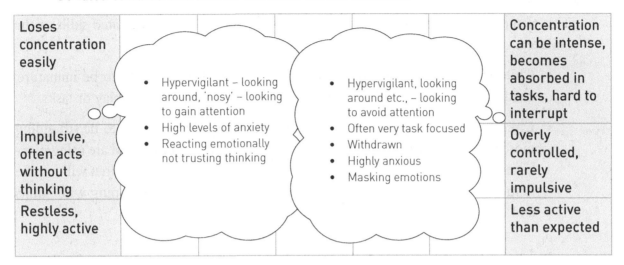

Play and task-related behaviours and relationships with peers

Section 2 of the checklist focuses on observation of the child in play and with peers, considering how ready the child is to focus away from his or her need of adult support and able to engage with and explore the social environment and the world of other children.

Children with attachment difficulties are generally emotionally more immature than their peers; although for some children this is masked by an apparent pseudomaturity, they appear older than their chronological age, that is, too grown up. These children may have immature social skills and need more adult support to engage with their peers.

Behaviour with other children

This element structures the observation to consider whether children are interested or not interested in relating with their peers.

- Children who are interested in relating with their peers, but perhaps not competent socially to do this, will be rated more on the left-hand side of the observation checklist. They will need more structure, supervision and support to help them develop prosocial skills and learn to interact successfully with peers.

- Children who are not interested in relating with their peers will be rated more on the right-hand side of the observation checklist. Consideration needs to be given as to whether these children are ready for peer relationships, but need additional support, or whether their level of immaturity means that they still need adult relationships which will later be used to explore the world of peer relationships.

Play and task-related behaviour

This element structures the observation to consider the play or task-related skills of the children.

- Children rated to the left of the observation checklist are likely to be immature, needing more play-based activities and more adult support with play or tasks.

- Children rated to the right of the observation checklist are likely to be struggling more with relationships, whether with adults or other children, and are using play- or task-focused behaviours to avoid these relationships. These children will require help and support to build confidence in their relationships, beginning with adults and then extending to other children.

Behaviour with other children

This illustration provides guidance on observations you might make in relation to the child's behaviour with other children that might suggest he or she should be rated towards one side or the other on the checklist.

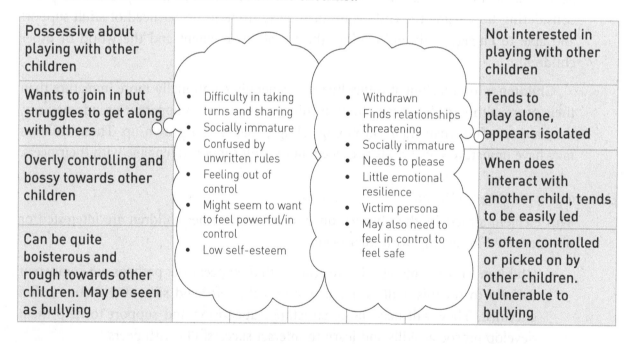

Possessive about playing with other children		**Not interested in playing with other children**
Wants to join in but struggles to get along with others	• Difficulty in taking turns and sharing • Socially immature • Confused by unwritten rules • Feeling out of control • Might seem to want to feel powerful/in control • Low self-esteem	• Withdrawn • Finds relationships threatening • Socially immature • Needs to please • Little emotional resilience • Victim persona • May also need to feel in control to feel safe	**Tends to play alone, appears isolated**
Overly controlling and bossy towards other children		**When does interact with another child, tends to be easily led**
Can be quite boisterous and rough towards other children. May be seen as bullying		**Is often controlled or picked on by other children. Vulnerable to bullying**

Play and task-related behaviour

This illustration provides guidance on observations you might make in relation to the child's play and task-related behaviour that might suggest he or she should be rated towards one side or the other on the checklist.

Attachment behaviours

Section 3 of the checklist allows you to match observations to attachment styles of relating that the child might bring in to the classroom. Understanding the style of relating that children habitually use with adults in the classroom can provide important information to guide ways of working with the children. Chapters 9 and 10 provide further information about attachment behaviours in school to help interpret observations in this section.

This is not an assessment of attachment difficulty or disorder but an observation of style of relating. Do not worry if observations do not match easily to one of the attachment patterns; some children tend to relate with a single style while other children use a range of styles.

This section allows you to think about whether a child's style leans towards secure, avoidant or ambivalent (or a combination of these). Children with more serious attachment difficulties (those described as having disorganized-controlling attachment styles of relating) will also show these basic styles, but the level of the control that they exert in their relationships is greater. As a rule of thumb, children who are rated as 'sometimes' are likely to be demonstrating insecurity in their relationship style, while those who are rated predominantly as 'almost always' are likely to be demonstrating the more controlling patterns of relating.

In this section of the checklist you are guided to observe the child in a number of situations which are likely to reveal his or her habitual attachment style of relating with others.

How is the child upon separation and reunion with caregiver?

Separations and reunions are times when children's attachment needs can get easily activated. It is therefore helpful to observe children's behaviour at these times.

How does the child behave with familiar and unfamiliar adults?

Children often generalize the behaviour they use with familiar caregivers to their interactions with other adults in their life, but this can vary depending upon how stressed or relaxed they are within these interactions. Observing children with a range of adults can therefore give some indication about both the attachment patterns they display as well as how stressful they find these interactions. Generally children will display attachment behaviours within relationships that they find more stressful.

How does the child behave when experiencing minor hurts?

Attachment behaviours are activated when children experience increased stress. This serves the purpose of orientating the child towards the caregiver in order to obtain comfort and soothing. For children with insecure attachments this reveals itself in less obvious comfort-seeking behaviours. Self-reliance to maintain closeness, attention-needing at times of low stress and controlling behaviours are all complex ways of reducing stress in children who find it difficult to seek comfort in straightforward ways. To observe attachment and comfort-seeking behaviours it is therefore helpful to watch children at times of increased stress. Experiencing minor physical hurts (e.g. bumps and falls) or psychological hurts (e.g. experiencing conflict with another child) will increase stress for a child.

For each of these situations you can consider the behaviour being observed in relation to the child's attachment style. Thus:

- *Secure attachment pattern:* children will predominantly be rated as 'like any other child of the same age'.

- *Avoidant attachment pattern:* children who are self-reliant (appearing not to need their caregiver or the adults in school) are anxious to please or unusually compliant. These children will be rated on the right-hand side more than the left based on observations.

- *Ambivalent attachment pattern:* children who are clingy, attention-needing and more emotionally demanding. These children will be rated on the left-hand side more than the right based on observations.

How is the child upon separation and reunion with caregiver?

This illustration provides guidance on observations you might make in relation to a child's behaviour on separation and reunion with the caregiver that might suggest he or she should be rated towards one side or the other on the checklist.

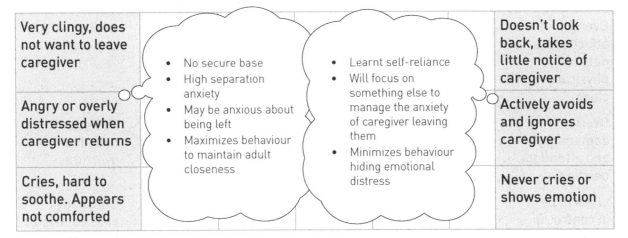

How does the child behave with familiar adults?

This illustration provides guidance on observations you might make in relation to the child's behaviour with familiar adults that might suggest he or she should be rated towards one side or the other on the checklist.

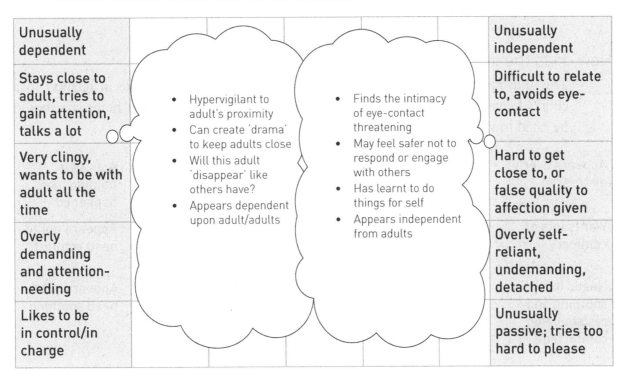

How does the child behave with unfamiliar adults?

This illustration provides guidance on observations you might make in relation to the child's behaviour with unfamiliar adults that might suggest he or she should be rated towards one side or the other on the checklist.

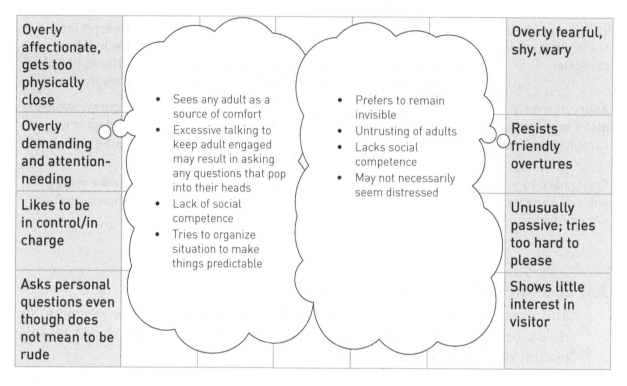

Overly affectionate, gets too physically close		**Overly fearful, shy, wary**
Overly demanding and attention-needing		**Resists friendly overtures**
Likes to be in control/in charge		**Unusually passive; tries too hard to please**
Asks personal questions even though does not mean to be rude		**Shows little interest in visitor**

Left cloud:
- Sees any adult as a source of comfort
- Excessive talking to keep adult engaged may result in asking any questions that pop into their heads
- Lack of social competence
- Tries to organize situation to make things predictable

Right cloud:
- Prefers to remain invisible
- Untrusting of adults
- Lacks social competence
- May not necessarily seem distressed

How does the child behave when experiencing minor hurts?

This illustration provides guidance on observations you might make in relation to a child's behaviour when experiencing minor hurts that might suggest he or she should be rated towards one side or the other on the checklist.

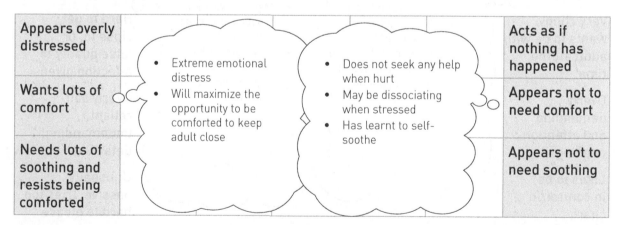

Appears overly distressed		**Acts as if nothing has happened**
Wants lots of comfort		**Appears not to need comfort**
Needs lots of soothing and resists being comforted		**Appears not to need soothing**

Left cloud:
- Extreme emotional distress
- Will maximize the opportunity to be comforted to keep adult close

Right cloud:
- Does not seek any help when hurt
- May be dissociating when stressed
- Has learnt to self-soothe

Emotional state

Section 4 of the checklist has been designed to aid observation of emotional state, and the way that this emotion is displayed through feelings.

It is likely that, with the stress of being in school and the need to relate to a range of adults and children that the child will adopt emotional displays learnt at home with early carers. Where these early relationships are experienced as insecure or stressful, these styles of relating can place the child at a disadvantage in the school.

Children with attachment difficulties are often more emotionally immature than their peers. They have learnt to display emotions in a way that is adaptive, in that it helps them to feel safer in situations where they are feeling unsafe, but can appear dysfunctional, not helpful for them, and different compared to typically developing peers.

Current emotional state, considering any current circumstances?

Think about the main emotional state that the child is displaying. For example, does the child appear happy, sad, worried, frightened or angry? This may be very clear from the way the child displays his or her feelings, or you may need to think about the way he or she is behaving. For example, a child who is following you around all the time may be feeling anxious, or a child who is hiding may be feeling frightened.

Take into account any relevant context. For example, if the child is new to the classroom or has significant events happening at home, some display of anxiety or worry would be normal. Similarly a child who is generally a bit shy or slow to warm up might be expected to appear more anxious or sensitive upon arrival at the school.

Observe the child over a number of days to understand the predominant emotional state of the child.

How does the child display feelings?

A child's emotional state is not necessarily displayed in a straightforward way. This section allows you to reflect on the way that the child is generally displaying his or her feelings.

Questions to consider

- Does the child appear happy, sad, angry or anxious within the school?

- Does the child appear to express how he or she is feeling or do you think some feelings are hidden from view?

- Does the child find it difficult to cope with some of his or her feelings, perhaps taking this out on self or others?

- Do you think that the child's emotional displays indicate that he or she needs more emotional support than a typical child?

- Do you think that the child's lack of emotional display indicates that he or she needs more emotional support than a typical child?

Current emotional state, considering any current circumstances?

This illustration provides guidance on observations you might make in relation to the child's current emotional state that might suggest he or she should be rated towards one side or the other on the checklist.

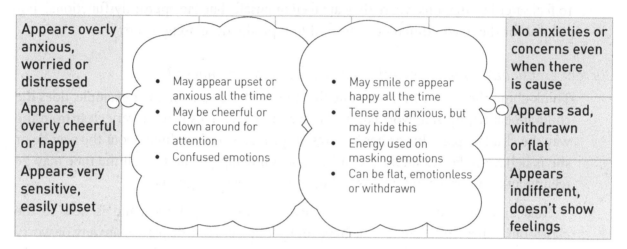

How does the child display feelings?

This illustration provides guidance on observations you might make in relation to the child's display of feelings that might suggest he or she should be rated towards one side or the other on the checklist.

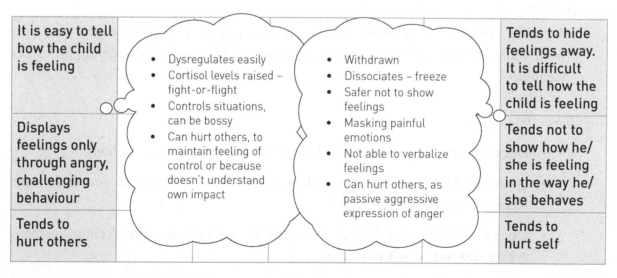

Attitude to attendance at school

This final section of the checklist provides an opportunity to observe the child's general ability to cope in the school. Children rated either to the left or to the right are likely to be immature and requiring additional adult support, although the way that this is demonstrated varies from child to child.

While children who are timid or disruptive tend to be easily noticed, be careful to also notice the child who copes with insecurity by being pseudomature (rather too grown up), or 'too good to be true'. These children are also in need of additional support.

Attitude to attendance at school

This illustration provides guidance on observations you might make in relation to the child's attitude to attendance that might suggest he or she should be rated towards one side or the other on the checklist.

Overly enthusiastic about attending	Extreme separation anxiety · May be articulate but doesn't easily understand social inferences/rules · May want to control their environment to get predictability	Easy to get lost in the crowd · Keep your head down · Invisible · Social incompetence · Pseudomaturity	Overly reluctant to attend
Does not cope well with school, appears immature			Copes well with school, but rather too grown up
Can become very disruptive or oppositional when directed by adults			Passive but non-compliant when directed by adults

Summary: tips for completion of checklist

- It may be helpful to have a child in mind who is of similar age and developmental stage when making observations of a child. This will provide a useful guide for the observer with regard to a typical child, that is, a child who would be recorded in the central column on the checklist. The observed child can then be compared to this 'typical child'.

- If a child is new to the school, the observer may be advised to wait a month to ensure that the child has had a chance to settle into the setting and that the staff are familiar with the child.

- Ideally the key person or a practitioner who knows the child well will complete the checklist. These observations can be part of the ongoing observations being made of the child. This member of staff may also need time to make additional observations of the child to inform the accurate completion of the checklist.

- Although the checklist assists the observer to make a structured observation, be careful not to simply observe the child as a 'snapshot'. It is more helpful if the checklist is used as a reflective tool. Think about a typical day for the child in the school while going through each section.

- Look at each row as a whole question, with the central column as the age typical indicator.

- The question offers contrasting examples of behaviour. Don't worry if the child demonstrates behaviour at both ends of the row. Simply tick both.

- It's useful to write some examples of behaviours, or triggers if known, in the comments space. This can be used later to identify targets for an action plan or individual education plan.

6 Worked Examples of the Observation Checklist

CHLOE AND JACOB

Following on from Chapters 4 and 5 on how to carry out the observations, this chapter has worked examples to show you how the checklist has been used for two children, Chloe and Jacob.

Worked example of the observation checklist 1: Chloe

Chloe's class teacher is concerned about Chloe. She is in Year 4, aged eight years. She is having difficulties engaging with numeracy and her progress in this area has stalled significantly. It is recognized that she has potential in numeracy, but Chloe seems unable to recognize that she has any numeracy skills and appears to have great difficulty in using them. In lessons she often refuses to take part in activities, saying that she can not do them and seems to put up a wall that stops her accepting encouragement and support to try activities.

Chloe's teacher feels that she needs to provide further support to help Chloe with her basic numeracy skills and to help her to be more organized in lessons so that she may be able to engage more easily and readily. However, the teacher is also aware that Chloe's difficulties in numeracy appear to be linked to a lot of anxiety around the subject. In addition there are signs apparent that she is experiencing an increased level of anxiety and need for attention throughout the school day – for example, she frequently calls out, makes noises and frequently seeks out the attention of her class teacher and teaching assistant. The teacher therefore completes an observation checklist to better understand Chloe's emotional difficulties.

1. Behaviour

		Almost always	Sometimes	As child of same age or stage of development	Sometimes	Almost always
What is child's behaviour like?	Resists boundaries, non-compliant		✓			Overly compliant, accepts boundaries with little fuss
	Difficult behaviour that is overly challenging				✓	Passive but difficult behaviour that is expressed subtly
	Unpredictable, easily triggered emotional outbursts		✓			Appears very self-contained, too good
Attention, concentration and activity levels?	Loses concentration easily	✓				Concentration can be intense, becomes absorbed in tasks, hard to interrupt
	Impulsive, often acts without thinking		✓			Overly controlled, rarely impulsive
	Restless, highly active		✓			Less active than expected

Although Chloe's behaviour is not overly challenging to staff around her, she appears to frequently lose concentration and is on occasions resistant to boundaries, has occasional emotional outbursts and will sometimes appear to be restless and highly active. As the ticks on the checklist tend to the left-hand side, it appears that in school Chloe tends towards an ambivalent attachment style of relating, leading her to need the attention and support of the adults around her to feel settled and safe. When this attention is not available she becomes more anxious and hypervigilant, thus being unable to concentrate and finding regulating her emotions difficult.

2. Play and task-related behaviours and relationships with peers

		Almost always	Sometimes	As child of same age or stage of development	Sometimes	Almost always	
Behaviour with other children	Possessive about playing with other children			✓			Not interested in playing or interacting with other children
	Wants to join in but struggles to get along with others		✓				Tends to play alone, appears isolated
	Overly controlling and bossy with other children				✓		When does interact with another child tends to be easily led
	Can be quite boisterous and rough towards other children. May be seen as bullying				✓		Is often controlled or picked on by other children. Vulnerable to bullying
Play and task-related behaviour	Reluctant to engage in new play or tasks				✓		Overly enthusiastic about new play or tasks
	Finds it difficult to settle to task	✓					Tends to get over-involved in task to exclusion of others
	Unable to play imaginatively			✓			Overly absorbed in imaginary world
	Overly competitive, always wants to be first		✓				Overly timid, reluctant to join in

This section of the checklist shows a mixed picture. Chloe appears less interested in relating to her peers compared to a typical child and needs support to develop peer relationships. Chloe's play behaviour is immature, needing more adult support.

Chloe sometimes struggles to get along with others and she may be easily led or controlled by others on occasions. Chloe can sometimes be over-excited about a task and might become competitive, frequently wanting to be first or win games, struggling a little and needing support when this is not the case.

Again in this section, it is very apparent that Chloe tends to frequently struggle with settling to a task.

3. Attachment behaviours

		Almost always	Sometimes	As child of same age or stage of development	Sometimes	Almost always	
How is the child upon separation and reunion with caregiver?	Very clingy, does not want to leave caregiver			✓			Doesn't look back, takes little notice of caregiver
	Angry or overly distressed when caregiver returns			✓			Actively avoids and ignores caregiver
	Cries, hard to soothe. Appears not comforted			✓			Never cries or shows emotion
How does the child behave with familiar adults?	Unusually dependent		✓				Unusually independent
	Stays close to adult, tries to gain attention, talks a lot	✓					Difficult to relate to, avoids eye-contact
	Very clingy, wants to be with adult all the time		✓				Hard to get close to, or false quality to affection given
	Overly demanding and attention-needing		✓				Overly self-reliant, undemanding, detached
	Likes to be in control/in charge				✓		Unusually passive; tries too hard to please

		Almost always	Sometimes	As child of same age or stage of development	Sometimes	Almost always	
How does the child behave with unfamiliar adults?	Overly affectionate, gets too physically close	✓					Overly fearful, shy, wary
	Overly demanding and attention-needing	✓					Resists friendly overtures
	Likes to be in control/in charge				✓		Unusually passive; tries too hard to please
	Asks personal questions even though does not mean to be rude			✓			Shows little interest in visitor
How does the child behave when experiencing minor hurts?	Appears overly distressed			✓			Acts as if nothing has happened
	Wants lots of comfort			✓			Appears not to need comfort
	Needs lots of soothing and resists being comforted			✓			Appears not to need soothing

Chloe appears to experience security with her parents, but demonstrates more anxiety when away from them. This means that the ticks in this section of the checklist tend to be spread, but there is a trend towards Chloe showing behaviours that are consistent with her tending to show a more ambivalent attachment style of relating in school. Chloe needs a substitute attachment figure to help her cope with school and being away from her parents. This leads her to need support and attention from her teachers to feel safe and settled and able to engage fully in learning. Key points in this section came from the ticks which were on the extreme left of the checklist – indicating that Chloe tends to stay close to an adult and engages him or her by talking a lot and, compared to her peers in the class, being overly demanding and attention-needing.

4. Emotional state

		Almost always	Sometimes	As child of same age or stage of development	Sometimes	Almost always	
Current emotional state, considering any current circumstances?	Appears overly anxious, worried or distressed		✓				No anxieties or concerns even when there is cause
	Appears overly cheerful or happy		✓				Appears sad, withdrawn or flat
	Appears very sensitive, easily upset				✓		Appears indifferent, doesn't show feelings
How does the child display feelings?	It is easy to tell how the child is feeling				✓		Tends to hide feelings away. It is difficult to tell how the child is feeling
	Displays feelings only through angry, challenging behaviour				✓		Tends not to show how he/she is feeling in the way he/she behaves
	Tends to hurt others			✓			Tends to hurt self

The ticks in this section of the checklist again present a mixed picture of Chloe's emotional needs in this area. Chloe can present as a child who hides feelings and sometimes it is hard to determine how she is feeling. This may be because she needs a little help to recognize the times when she feels anxious and support to express how she feels. She may need encouragement to seek support to help her to feel secure again. In contrast Chloe sometimes appears overly worried or distressed, or overly happy and cheerful – her teacher was able to identify that at these times Chloe struggles to be able to talk about her feelings and to identify strategies to help her to feel more calm and settled. She needs help to enable her to express her feelings more effectively.

5. Attitude to attendance at school

		Almost always	Sometimes	As child of same age or stage of development	Sometimes	Almost always	
Attitude to attendance at school	Overly enthusiastic about attending			✓			Overly reluctant to attend
	Does not cope well with school, appears immature		✓				Copes well with school, but rather too grown up
	Can become very disruptive or oppositional when directed by adults				✓		Passive but non-compliant when directed by adults

This section also supports the thought that Chloe is experiencing general anxiety about school and is on occasions appearing not to cope well with school. She can present as emotionally immature, especially when taking part in activities where she may be unsure or does not have support.

Taking the overall picture gleaned from the checklist, it is clear that Chloe is frequently attention-needing in school and can often show signs of anxiety. This anxiety is particularly apparent to teachers when it comes to taking part in numeracy lessons, but the checklist reveals a more pervasive pattern of anxiety in school.

Worked example of the observation checklist 2: Jacob

This case study illustrates the use of the checklist with a young boy, Jacob, living in foster care. The checklist was first used when Jacob came into care (marked as a tick). He was attending a nursery setting and the checklist was used as a focus and conversation tool with staff. These initial observations demonstrated the link between his behaviour and attachment needs.

The checklist was used again 18 months later (marked as a cross). At this time Jacob had changed placement and had also moved to Year 1 at school. The checklist helped staff to monitor Jacob's behaviour, and to link this to his high level of emotional need. The second observation clearly shows the detrimental impact the changes at home and school have had, in comparison with the first observation.

In this example we have indicated the two different time periods with two different symbols. However, the observer may prefer to use different colours for clarity.

1. Behaviour

WHAT IS JACOB'S BEHAVIOUR LIKE?

		Almost always	Sometimes	As child of same age or stage of development	Sometimes	Almost always	
What is child's behaviour like?	Resists boundaries, non-compliant	✘		✔			Overly compliant, accepts boundaries with little fuss
	Difficult behaviour that is overly challenging	✘	✔				Passive but difficult behaviour that is expressed subtly
	Unpredictable, easily triggered emotional outbursts	✘	✔				Appears very self-contained, too good

In the second observation Jacob is finding school a huge source of stress. He arrives at school already very tense, coming in very loud, very energetic and is almost on the verge of dysregulating. Thus any positive learnt behaviours from his time at nursery, such as coming into class appropriately have been overridden by his survival need to take control of this stressful situation. He has also learnt from his early experiences and initial school career that refusing to do as he is asked, and getting into others' personal space will meet his needs in some way. He doesn't feel secure enough to take on the challenges of what is expected of him. He is making sure that the adults will attend to him. 'Notice me; help me do any tiny, little task because I don't feel safe enough to attempt it by myself.'

JACOB'S ATTENTION, CONCENTRATION AND ACTIVITY LEVELS

		Almost always	Sometimes	As child of same age or stage of development	Sometimes	Almost always	
Attention, concentration and activity levels?	Loses concentration easily	✗	✓				Concentration can be intense, becomes absorbed in tasks, hard to interrupt
	Impulsive, often acts without thinking	✓ ✗					Overly controlled, rarely impulsive
	Restless, highly active	✗	✓				Less active than expected

Jacob has always struggled with concentration and impulsivity. At the second observation Jacob's ability to be able to concentrate on tasks is overtaken by his hyper-awareness to the proximity of the adult. His impulsivity is indicative of a much younger child. His executive function is not working well because of this immaturity, and the fear state he is in. In other words it is difficult for Jacob to feel calm enough to think and problem solve.

Children who have disrupted attachments often have sensory integration issues. This can result in the need to constantly move or fidget and can be helped by putting in strategies to deal with this.

2. Play and task-related behaviours and relationships with peers
JACOB'S BEHAVIOUR WITH OTHER CHILDREN

		Almost always	Sometimes	As child of same age or stage of development	Sometimes	Almost always	
Behaviour with other children	Possessive about playing with other children		✔ ✘				Not interested in playing with other children
	Wants to join in but struggles to get along with others	✔ ✘					Tends to play alone, appears isolated
	Overly controlling and bossy with other children	✘					When does interact with another child, tends to be easily led
	Can be quite boisterous and rough towards other children. May be seen as bullying	✘	✔				Is often controlled or picked on by other children. Vulnerable to bullying

Jacob is interested in relating to peers but has difficulty interacting with them. Although he is not overly possessive about playing with others, he finds it hard to take turns. Sometimes he is happier parallel playing; he wants to join in but is unsure of the unwritten rules. This leads to a lack of understanding; he knows something isn't right, but doesn't have the skills to repair it. This leads to feeling out of control. So, in order to feel better about himself he will take control. He can use his imagination but this is limited to his experiences. He often likes to be an animal so that he can be cared for. However, he likes to call the shots too and often doesn't take kindly to other children's ideas. This can be interpreted as bullying.

JACOB'S PLAY AND TASK-RELATED BEHAVIOUR

		Almost always	Sometimes	As child of same age or stage of development	Sometimes	Almost always	
Play and task-related behaviour	Reluctant to engage in new play or tasks		✓ ✗				Overly enthusiastic about new play or tasks
	Finds it difficult to settle to task	✗		✓			Tends to get over-involved in task to exclusion of others
	Unable to play imaginatively	✓			✗		Overly absorbed in imaginary world
	Overly competitive, always wants to be first		✗		✓		Overly timid, reluctant to join in

Jacob remains reluctant to engage in new tasks or play. Play skills are immature. At the second observation he is finding it harder to settle and has become more competitive.

Jacob needs an adult beside him, encouraging and supporting him in order for him to cope with the transition into a new activity and to attempt what is asked of him. He prefers to play as he finds academic tasks too challenging. He will need support to take baby steps to independent working.

From being unable to play imaginatively, he now sometimes becomes over-absorbed in his own world. This world can sometimes be much safer than the one he lives in. If he stays in that world, he doesn't have to come out and attempt the challenge required of him. He may need support in the transition from this type of play to the next task.

In nursery, Jacob occasionally didn't feel secure enough to join in or take part in games; he has found during this time that by taking control and wanting to be first or 'top dog' (as his teacher described it), he feels better about himself. Therefore, he is now demonstrating a competitive tendency. He finds other boys a threat to his self-worth. He has to compare himself to them, whereas, he has found that he can often 'beat' the girls because he is faster, stronger and bigger than them.

3. Attachment behaviours

HOW IS JACOB UPON SEPARATION AND REUNION WITH CAREGIVER?

		Almost always	Sometimes	As child of same age or stage of development	Sometimes	Almost always	
How is the child upon separation and reunion with caregiver?	Very clingy, does not want to leave caregiver			✓ ✗			Doesn't look back, takes little notice of caregiver
	Angry or overly distressed when caregiver returns			✓ not observed			Actively avoids and ignores caregiver
	Cries, hard to soothe. Appears not comforted		✗		✓		Never cries or shows emotion

When discussing this section with the teacher, it became apparent that Jacob gives off many mixed messages. On entering school, the teacher felt that Jacob craves a lot of attention from his carer and teachers. He always comes into school very loudly – shouting and invading the personal space of all the adults. His behaviour is such that the school adults have to remind him of the 'coming into school routine'. Once the carer has left, Jacob is very anxious and finds it hard to settle.

HOW DOES JACOB BEHAVE WITH FAMILIAR ADULTS?

		Almost always	Sometimes	As child of same age or stage of development	Sometimes	Almost always	
How does the child behave with familiar adults?	Unusually dependent			✓		✗	Unusually independent
	Stays close to adult, tries to gain attention, talks a lot				✓	✗	Difficult to relate to, avoids eye-contact
	Very clingy, wants to be with adult all the time			✓	✗		Hard to get close to, or false quality to affection given
	Overly demanding and attention-needing		✗		✓		Overly self-reliant, undemanding, detached
	Likes to be in control/in charge	✗	✓				Unusually passive; tries too hard to please

The second observation shows a pattern of increasing insecurity with familiar adults. Jacob deals with this not only through self-reliance and avoiding relationship but also through an increase in controlling and attention-needing behaviours.

The teacher also feels that Jacob's interactions are often insincere and are only to get the adult's attention. This was discussed as mixed messaging. Jacob is unsure of how to express his needs so will appear attention-seeking, whereby he is actually saying, 'I'm not sure I can trust you, I can't invest in a relationship but by getting your attention that will suffice. I only know surface relationships and haven't learnt that reciprocal interactions give true depth to social interactions.'

HOW DOES JACOB BEHAVE WITH UNFAMILIAR ADULTS?

		Almost always	Sometimes	As child of same age or stage of development	Sometimes	Almost always	
How does the child behave with unfamiliar adults?	Overly affectionate, gets too physically close			✗	✓		Overly fearful, shy, wary
	Overly demanding and attention-needing		✗	✓			Resists friendly overtures
	Likes to be in control/in charge	✗	✓				Unusually passive; tries too hard to please
	Asks personal questions even though does not mean to be rude				✗	✓	Shows little interest in visitor

From showing little interest in unfamiliar adults while in nursery, Jacob now looks for comfort from most adults, familiar or otherwise. After a few visits Jacob is visibly hyper-aroused by the presence of visitors. For example, he will circle the room, refusing to sit down at the table or carpet area where the visitor is sitting. He does start to interact with the visitor after he or she has been in the room for a while. He continues to show a lack of trust around adults.

HOW DOES JACOB BEHAVE WHEN EXPERIENCING MINOR HURTS?

		Almost always	Sometimes	As child of same age or stage of development	Sometimes	Almost always	
How does the child behave when experiencing minor hurts?	Appears overly distressed	✘			✔		Acts as if nothing has happened
	Wants lots of comfort	✘			✔		Appears not to need comfort
	Needs lots of soothing and resists being comforted	✘			✔		Appears not to need soothing

Jacob's increase in insecurity is clearly seen in the second observation. If Jacob has a slight hurt, for instance a bruise on his leg from a knock the night before, he will limp excessively, won't be able to sit on the carpet and keeps rolling up his trousers to look at the injury. He keeps this attention to his injury all day. He will show it to any adult.

When looking at the complete table of attachment behaviours, it appears that Jacob has moved from being relatively secure, but with some insecure, avoidant attachment behaviours, to much increased insecurity, with more controlling and attention-needing behaviours. This demonstrates a move to a more ambivalent attachment style of relating. This move to increased dependence can be positive for a child who is too self-reliant. For example, a child who moves from extreme self-reliance to some attention-needing behaviours is seen as making progress in learning to use adults as a source of comfort and security. In Jacob's case the move from milder self-reliance to more extreme attention-needing behaviours reveals much increased anxiety and insecurity. This is consistent with changes at home and school which are very unsettling for Jacob. At home Jacob is not able to ascertain who his primary carer is, which leaves him confused and insecure. Therefore, he arrives at school clearly worried about who will be picking him up at the end of the day, where he will be going back to and the lack of routine and boundaries. He clearly feels out of control and is making great effort to gain some control of his disorganized world. He is also making sure that the adults around him don't forget him. Jacob is therefore reacting to the instability in his care environment and his attachment behaviour is becoming more disorganized and controlling as a consequence.

4. Emotional state

JACOB'S CURRENT EMOTIONAL STATE, CONSIDERING ANY CURRENT CIRCUMSTANCES?

		Almost always	Sometimes	As child of same age or stage of development	Sometimes	Almost always	
Current emotional state, considering any current circumstances?	Appears overly anxious, worried or distressed	✗			✓		No anxieties or concerns even when there is cause
	Appears overly cheerful or happy		✓ ✗				Appears sad, withdrawn or flat
	Appears very sensitive, easily upset	✗			✓		Appears indifferent, doesn't show feelings

In the second observation Jacob displays hyper-aroused behaviour for most of his time in school. He has moved from masking his feelings and rarely being able to show his anxieties to bordering on regular dysregulation. This frequently results in him escalating from refusing to comply with requests, 'fronting up' to adults, marching around the room, running out of the classroom to climbing up on tables and work surfaces.

Jacob complains and whinges a lot and at times cries very easily when trying to explain himself. His language difficulties are exacerbated by his anxious state when it gets to this point. This has on occasions heightened his frustration.

HOW DOES JACOB DISPLAY FEELINGS?

		Almost always	Sometimes	As child of same age or stage of development	Sometimes	Almost always	
How does the child display feelings?	It is easy to tell how the child is feeling				✗	✓	Tends to hide feelings away. It is difficult to tell how the child is feeling
	Displays feelings only through angry, challenging behaviour	✗			✓		Tends not to show how he/she is feeling in the way he/she behaves
	Tends to hurt others	✓	✗				Tends to hurt self

This is an area of continuing difficulty for Jacob. Although the teacher has ticked the box stating that Jacob tends to hide his feelings away, in discussion it was felt that this was due to him not being able to verbalize his feelings correctly. In fact protective behaviour work was included in an action plan and this quickly established that Jacob has little understanding of what basic emotions are.

Jacob has also learnt that he gets a reaction to invading others' personal space. He is a tall lad for his age and is finding that using a more physical approach with his peers and some adults will give him his own way, even if it is inappropriate. This is giving him a sense of being powerful, which in turn makes him feel better about himself, regardless of the fact that other children will avoid him or his friendship groups may be limited.

Adults in the nurture group react to Jacob's aggressive behaviour with calmness and gently support him to more appropriate behaviours. However, unfamiliar or untrained adults can react in different ways which can in turn increase Jacob's anxiety and behaviours.

5. Attitude to attendance at school

		Almost always	Sometimes	As child of same age or stage of development	Sometimes	Almost always	
Attitude to attendance at school	Overly enthusiastic about attending			✓	✗		Overly reluctant to attend
	Does not cope well with school, appears immature	✗		✓			Copes well with school, but rather too grown up
	Can become very disruptive or oppositional when directed by adults	✗			✓		Passive but non-compliant when directed by adults

Jacob is increasingly reluctant to attend school and his insecurity is evident through immature and disruptive behaviour.

In Chapter 8, we revisit Chloe and Jacob to see how the checklists are interpreted and what forms of support are set up.

7 Analysis of Information

INTERPRETING THE COMPLETED CHECKLIST

In this chapter interpretation of the checklist is discussed. This will consider how to interpret the profile that has been built up about a child, and how to use this interpretation to plan additional support which can meet the emotional and social needs identified.

When the checklist has been completed, it is helpful to initially look at each table's pattern of ticks before considering the observations for individual behaviours. Look at each section and consider first whether there is a pattern:

- Do the ticks lean towards a particular side – left or right?

- Are there more ticks down the centre of the page and only the odd one or two either side? Does this therefore just pinpoint some specific difficulties that can be addressed for the child?

- Alternatively, there may be a number of ticks that predominately lean towards one side or another, with a few ticks down the central column, suggesting that the child might need more comprehensive help.

- It can be helpful to work from the outside column into the centre. Look at the 'almost always' ticks first as the needs associated with these examples are often the most urgent to address.

- As a rule of thumb, if the majority of ticks lean towards the right of the central column look at insecure avoidant styles and strategies, and if the ticks incline towards the left look at the insecure ambivalent styles and strategies. When ticks appear on both ends a combination of strategies is likely to be helpful.

This pattern of ticks together with notes of behaviours or triggers observed then forms the basis of an analysis of the information. This allows a profile of the child to be developed, guiding ideas and strategies which might support the child within the school.

- Return to the detailed guidance provided in Chapter 5. This will help to identify the needs shown on the checklist, and explain the relevance of where the ticks are positioned.

- Keep reading this section alongside the other chapters to plan how you are going to support the child using an attachment-led approach.

- Remember it is important to recognize the child that internalizes his or her emotions, the 'too good' child, as well as the child whose behaviour can be seen explicitly.

- Consider whether the child's behaviour would seem appropriate in a younger child, that is, is the child demonstrating immaturity? Conversely, does the child appear as an older child, that is, is the child too 'grown up' and independent (pseudomature)?

- Consider that all behaviours are a means of communication. Reflect on what is the hidden need that the child's behaviour may be expressing.

- Within the school, ensure that everyone has an understanding of the child's needs and responds consistently.

- Multiple observations can help chart the child's progress over time. One important factor to remember in filling in subsequent observations is the child's home circumstances. Have there been any significant changes? Do you suspect that these changes may be having an effect on the child's behaviour?

- It can be helpful to discuss the interpretation with other people who know the child. This can enrich the interpretations being made as the profile on the checklist is considered in the context of the experience of the child by the different people.

Knowledge of attachment experience and how this can impact on the way a child relates to adults and children within the school can help in interpreting the completed checklist. It is important to note, however, that this checklist is not an assessment of the child's attachment style. It cannot be used to diagnose attachment difficulties but it can increase awareness of the way secure and insecure patterns of attachment impact on the child's day-to-day functioning within the school. This may in turn affect how a child is communicating his or her needs through his or her behaviour.

A child with an avoidant style of attachment relating may appear to be doing well, appearing as an independent child who displays high levels of involvement in self-chosen activities and is secure in self-care skills. However, this child may miscue adults about the need for nurturing as he or she draws upon embedded self-reliant coping strategies from early life experiences. This self-reliance can look like successful independence, hiding the fact that he or she is actually feeling highly insecure. This child may need to learn to develop relationships; learning to be *dependent* on an adult (i.e. teacher or teaching assistant) before becoming independent. Apparent self-reliance is now seen as being 'too grown up' for the child's age (pseudomature).

A child with an ambivalent style of attachment relating may need to stay close to an adult to gain attention. The consequent behaviours that are displayed may be described by practitioners as challenging and 'attention-seeking'. The child miscues the adult, fearing the loss of attention that may come with exploration and learning. Well-meaning adults may try to encourage independence, and discourage displays of dependency failing to realize that the behaviours display 'attention-needing'. The child is demonstrating through his or her behaviour the need for reassurance that you can attend to his or her needs. Only then will the fear of abandonment reduce to the point that the child can begin to explore and learn.

Children who are showing extremes of these behaviours, appearing controlling, inflexible and rigid in their behaviours will be observed predominantly at the extremes on the checklist. They may also have times when these behavioural strategies break down as the child 'loses it' or becomes very shut down. These fight, flight or freeze reactions indicate that these children are more disorganized and controlling in their attachment style. These are the children who struggle most to feel safe within the school.

These insecure patterns of relating therefore communicate a continuing need to feel safe in the school, and to build trust in the relationship with a teacher or teaching assistant, who can help them to co-regulate their arousal levels (whether this is high or low). It is helpful in this context to understand that children who have experienced an insecure early life experience may be emotionally and socially younger than their chronological age.

Keep in mind four groups of questions when interpreting the checklist:

- What age group would best relate to the behaviours being observed? This emotional age is often consistently younger than the chronological age in children with emotional difficulties. How would you deal with a child of that age? Notice that at times of dysregulation or more extreme stress, these immature behaviours can spiral downwards, and the child's emotional age is now much younger than the chronological age. In helping the child, the teacher or teaching assistant will need to adjust to this shifting emotional age.

- Does the child feel safe or unsafe? Think about how you are making this judgement; what triggers can you identify that increase feelings of danger or restore feelings of safety? Consider how you might increase the feelings of safety for the child.

- How well is the child fitting in with classroom expectations? Think about the 'unwritten rules', ways of behaving that a child is expected to know about by the age they have reached and are therefore not made explicit. An immature child may need support to understand this. Has the child been specifically told about the expectations of the situation? Bear in mind, these children often have difficulties with inferences and abstract concepts and are visual learners.

- Are there any known triggers for the child being observed? Notice patterns to the behaviours that you are observing. Are there particular situations that seem to lead to habitual behaviours? Notice also exceptions to this, what has helped a child cope with a situation that he or she usually has difficulty with. Use this information to think about how triggers can be avoided or supported for the child.

Using the observations to inform an action plan

Once the observations are made and interpreted, these observations can be translated into clear targets and actions that will help to meet the needs identified. It is helpful to draw up a plan of action that practitioners might take to help the child. In this way the observations can guide the development of some clear ideas or strategies for helping the child (an action plan). Without this there is a danger that while understanding of the child has improved, this is not translated into improvements in meeting the needs identified. Developing an action plan which helps to tailor the support to the child's needs is therefore an important part of using the observation checklist to guide practice.

Generally the person who made the observations is best placed to write the action plan, perhaps in discussion with others involved in supporting the child. For example, it might be helpful to involve the special educational needs coordinator (SENCO) or the designated teacher for looked after children.

It is important to set a review date for this action plan in order to monitor whether the actions identified are helpful, and to adapt the action plan if they are not helping or in line with the progress that the child is making. Be careful not to reduce support too quickly, however; developing security in an insecure child can be a lengthy process.

An action plan template is included with the checklist for those who want to use it, although settings may have their own action plan template that they wish to use.

In addition to the action plan, it may be appropriate to complete a plan in line with the usual recording method of intervention within the school. For example, schools often develop individual education plans (IEPs), which are plans that are drawn up by the practitioner to help the school, together with the parent, to identify the child's needs and to ensure that particular difficulties are supported. Similar to the action plan described above, the IEP provides targets, actions for meeting these targets, who will take the action and how success will be measured. Actions that the parent can take to support the school might be included in this plan. Provision maps might be used by a school as an alternative to the IEP. This is a more succinct way of listing interventions and identifying who, where and what will be done to support the child.

Any of these plans can be used to identify targets for providing increased social and emotional support to the child, interventions that can be implemented in order to meet these targets, and ways of reviewing the targets in order to establish whether the plan has been successful or not. This can include further periods of observation using the checklist. This in turn can lead to revision of the action plan.

To support the child's continuing social and emotional development, some children are also placed on 'School Action Plus' as staff seek the involvement of other services to ensure that the child's needs are met (for example, a child with identified expressive speech difficulties might be supported with the help of the Speech, Language and Communication Service).

If the child's emotional and social needs are particularly severe, further funding may be sought to ensure that these needs are met. Such funding can ensure the provision of input from professionals external to the school, as well as providing the means to increase the staff to pupil ratio so that the child with particular difficulties can be better supported. For example, this support might enable the child's key person to build a relationship with the child so that a child's emotional needs are met. This enables the child to feel both physically and emotionally safe and able to begin to explore all the activities available in the school.

The structured observations informed by the checklist can provide important information to evidence this need. Within the UK there are several potential sources of support and funding, such as the Early Years and Child Care Service Inclusion Team and Special Education Needs Services. Such services may consider requests for funding to provide additional support either in the early years setting or as the child transfers into school.

Implementing the action plan

It is helpful if the action plan can be implemented by a teacher or teaching assistant working with the child, supported by other staff in the school. Often the key person is already identified and has been involved in completing the checklist. However, sometimes the need for a key person to work with the child might be identified through the use of the checklist. In this case it is important to think about who in the school might be best suited to be the child's key person and how this person is going to establish a relationship with the child or in many cases how he or she can enhance a relationship that already exists. Consideration needs to be given to the level of support that the child is likely to need while in the setting, how to give the teacher or teaching assistant time to provide this support and how this can be funded. This investment in time and resources is key to supporting the child with emotional difficulties.

Putting in appropriate strategies can help to provide an environment for a child that is attuned to his or her needs, but there is no quick fix. Sometimes behaviours will continue and staff will have to take encouragement from the smallest of improvements. Additionally a strategy may work for a while but then the child changes tactics. A rethink of approach is needed. As the staff continue to understand and work with the child, and are able to adjust to the child's changing needs, security will be built and slowly, over time progress will be seen.

In Chapter 8 we return to Chloe and Jacob in order to illustrate how the observation checklist can be used to provide clear ideas for interventions which will support the needs identified. Examples of completed action plans are included to provide an illustration of how the checklist can lead to specific ideas for helping the child, including details of what is needed, how this need can be met and who will have responsibility for implementing these ideas.

Consequences of implementing an action plan

One outcome of working with the observation checklist is that the teacher's curiosity about why the child behaves as he or she does, and what the behaviour is communicating, is increased. This is very helpful as it increases understanding and helps the teacher to be more in tune with what the child needs.

As the action plan is implemented, the practitioners will continue to develop a relationship with the child and to develop further understanding about this child. For example, in observing how the child responds to the interventions that are implemented, behaviours might become better understood. Triggers to behaviours may also become more apparent. It might be noticed that when a child is more challenged by an activity that his or her stress levels increase. This in turn leads to the child having increased difficulty within the peer group, perhaps because his or her controlling behaviours towards other children increases. The practitioner now understands that when the child is more controlling and less able to share and cooperate it is likely that stress has increased. Activities that reduce stress might be helpful for the child at this point. In this way strategies that work well for this child are identified and further refined.

It is important that the key person or practitioner working with the child continues to be curious and to develop a deeper understanding of the child. Be careful, however, about asking children why they have done something. Some tentative questioning with the older child might be helpful, but generally being asked 'why' reinforces for children that they have been naughty in some way. This often compounds the shame felt by the child, and thus can strengthen unhelpful behaviours. Wondering aloud, helping the child to make sense of his or her experience, can be more helpful than questioning the child on why he or she is doing something. For example, 'Jake is very wobbly today, I am wondering if he is worrying that his mum may not collect him at home time.' 'Stephanie is very cross with Alex today, I wonder if she is unhappy because he has been chosen as monitor today and she hasn't. It is hard not to have special things for yourself.'

Changes within the child over time are not always straightforward. Sometimes a child may make little progress. This may indicate that changes to the action plan are needed. The strategies being implemented are perhaps not as helpful as was hoped. For example, it may have been decided to help a child who is struggling to separate from his or her parent at the beginning of the day by including the parent in the first activity. However, it is noticed that the child is increasingly preoccupied about when the parent is leaving, and therefore is not settling into the class as hoped. In this case a change to the plan might be considered. Perhaps instead of the parent coming in, the key person goes out to meet and greet the child, allowing the child to experience the parent and key person working together to help the child make the transition from the parent in to the classroom.

It is helpful not to make changes too quickly. It may be that a particular intervention will work given additional time. The staff need to hold firm to what they have planned, allowing a longer time within which to see progress.

There are two particular situations to be mindful about. First, children who initially came across as independent, possibly withdrawn and avoidant of relationships may suddenly start presenting as attention-needing as the action plan is implemented. The child becomes more dependent, changing from a child who was causing little trouble in class to a child who is demanding of staff time and energy. Staff can be left thinking that they have done things wrong and created a monster! It can be difficult, under these circumstances, to recognize that the child's needs are beginning to be fulfilled. It may be tempting to stop the interventions in the hope that the child returns to his or her previous, more manageable mode of behaving. *This must not happen!* Staff will need to understand that this swing in behaviours is all part of the relationship-building, trust and feeling of safety that the child will be experiencing. As children become more able to seek relationships with adults, they start to make up for experiences they have previously missed. This increased dependency and neediness, if satisfied, will then allow them to return to an appropriate level of independence, but this time the independence will be healthy as children develop autonomy in the context of being able to seek support when needed. If we let children down at this stage, the message to them will confirm that adults cannot be trusted, thus affecting their self-worth, self-esteem, confidence, relationships and ultimately their ability to explore and learn.

Second, remember to keep in mind the context the child is living within. Changes outside of school can have a big influence on the child in school. This will be reflected in changes on the checklist during subsequent observations, and will guide adjustments to the action plan to reflect changing needs. Without bearing in mind such context, the different observations can present a confusing picture. For example, a checklist was completed for a child who had just come into the care system (see the example of Jacob in Chapter 6). This first observation highlighted a number of predominately avoidant style behaviours that this child was displaying in his nursery setting. As the child moved in to a reception class, he also changed carer. In a second observation, his behaviour had escalated and the child now displayed more ambivalent/disorganized-controlling attachment behaviours. This changing relationship style in school reflected his changing care arrangements outside of school alongside moving into the reception year. It is important to look at the completed checklists with caution. This child is not making the shift from independence to dependence in a healthy manner but is showing his confusion of his situation and increasingly more desperate attempts to get his needs met in school. The behaviours he was displaying were rated predominantly as 'almost always', indicating that these behaviours reflected a disorganized-controlling relationship with people in his world rather than the more healthy need for attention that a previously avoidant child can display when he realizes that adults can be a source of support.

Implementation of the action plan continues to give staff important information about the child. Reviewing this plan and revisiting targets will build up an important profile of the child and what is helpful for him or her. Additionally the checklist can be revisited to monitor progress and to provide further information. This developing understanding will underpin successful support to the child. This information can then move with the child as he or she progresses through the school, ensuring good transitions and helping the child resettle and continue to benefit from the support that has been provided. New staff will want to do their own observations, but the past information will provide important context for these new observations.

Conclusion

The observation checklist can be a helpful tool for identifying the emotional and social difficulties a child is experiencing within school, and also for monitoring the progress the child is making over time. To be of maximum use the observations need to lead to clear ideas for supporting the emotional experience of the child, helping to reduce emotional distress and to support emotional development. This in turn will impact positively on the behaviour the child is displaying, the ability to manage the social relationships with adults and other children and it will improve the child's readiness to learn within school.

The following chapter revisits the cases of Chloe and Jacob, but before you read on, read the worked examples of the observation checklist once again and form your own interpretation of the findings – what kind of needs do you think they exhibit, and what forms of support would be appropriate? You may also want to leaf through some of the following chapters, which provide information on effective supports for children with attachment difficulties and other developmental challenges.

Summary: developing support

Reasons for using the checklist

- Concerns about behaviour.

- Concerns about child who is not achieving or managing socially.

- Baseline observation to compare child to over time.

- Desire to raise awareness of needs of child.

- Desire to monitor child through period of change or transition.

Collecting contextual information

- Background, early experience and current functioning.

- Knowledge and observations of child in school.

- Knowledge about the impact of parenting and attachment difficulties.

Interpreting checklist

- Look at pattern of ticks.

- Consider ticks at extreme, each side and in middle.

- Use this to build up a profile of the child.

- Relate to avoidant, ambivalent and controlling patterns of relating.

- What is emotional age of the child?

- Does the child feel safe or unsafe?

- Is the child fitting in with classroom expectations?

- Are there any observable triggers for the child's behaviours?

- Use notes to accompany checklist for extra guidance.

- Think about meaning underlying the behaviours.

- Relate to background information.

Developing an action plan

- Support an action plan with an individual education plan or provision map.

- Identify targets to increase social and emotional support.

- Develop interventions to meet targets.

- Plan how interventions will be reviewed.

- Plan further periods of observation.

- Revise action plan.

- Consider further action; placing child on Code of Practice, involving other services, securing additional funding.

Implementing the action plan

- Identify key person and support to build a relationship with child.

- Implement level of support needed for child.

- Implement strategies and monitor progress with these.

- Stay curious about the child and wonder aloud.

- Continue to support child who becomes more attention-needing.

- Notice when there are changes for the child outside of the school.

8
Worked Examples of Interpreting the Checklist and Support Plans

CHLOE AND JACOB

In this chapter we return to the worked examples of Chloe and Jacob. We explore how the interpretations of the observations made on the checklist were turned into action plans with clear goals, targets and interventions, so that the children's emotional needs could be better supported.

Chloe

Chloe was allocated a key adult, Mrs H, who as the class teaching assistant already had a positive relationship with Chloe. Mrs H was offered further training and support to develop strategies to use to help Chloe to feel more secure and less anxious in school. She learnt to spot times when Chloe may be feeling more anxious and developed ways to respond and support her more appropriately at these times. Strategies recommended included the use of relationship-based play and elements of protective behaviours.

Chloe's teacher and Mrs H then changed the way in which Chloe took part in numeracy sessions – going out of the classroom with Mrs H to take part in some relationship-based play activities before receiving the learning input from the numeracy session in a calm and supportive one-to-one manner. She then returned to the classroom to take part in the practical and recording activities with the rest of her peers – again with Mrs H's support.

Additionally a support teacher delivered six sessions of direct work to Chloe. In these sessions she worked to help Chloe to consider and recognize her own 'early warning signs' – the signs that her body gives to her when she is beginning to feel anxious, and helped her to develop strategies that will help her to begin to decrease her own anxiety and be able to take part in school in a more settled and successful way. The strategies covered with Chloe were shared with her teacher and Mrs H so that they could support her to use them in between visits by the support teacher.

Action Plan to Support Observation Checklist

Name of child	Chloe		DOB		Code of Practice
Dates of observation					None / (SA)
Involved professionals	Support teacher				SA+ / STATEMENT
What works well	Supportive task board to get reward for working independently Tasks on interactive whiteboard in order to follow more complex instructions Small chunks of praise, celebrating ideas with peers, peer compliments			Areas for development	Training for staff about attachment theory and its application in the classroom
Concern	Target	How will this be achieved?		Resources	Who? Where?
Chloe experiences increased anxiety in school This is not always recognized by staff	Staff who work with Chloe will develop a greater understanding of how they can support her to feel more secure and less anxious in school	Further training in attachment theory, and supporting children who are anxious in school		Purchase training course from Education Psychology Service	SENCO
Concern	Target	How will this be achieved?		Resources	Who? Where?
Chloes lacks confidence in numeracy	Chloe will begin to feel less anxious and more confident in her own abilities in numeracy. She will begin to readily take part in numeracy activities and begin to enjoy and achieve to her potential	Six sessions of direct work with Chloe using protective behaviours programme Changes to way numeracy is delivered to Chloe, including relationship-based play session prior to numeracy session		Quiet room Quiet room Use of relationship-based play-type activities	Support teacher Class teacher Teaching assistant
Review date		Action plan shared with		Parents Class teacher Support teacher Teaching assistant SENCO	

Chloe's class teacher and Mrs H soon noticed that the strategies that they and Chloe were using to help her to feel more secure and less anxious in school were having a very positive impact. Initially Chloe still needed some support to notice when she was experiencing anxiety and her early warning signs, but when she did notice she happily used strategies and started to appear more settled and happy in school and less needing of adult support and attention. As a result of the support that she was receiving, Chloe was also starting to be able to access and take part in more and more numeracy activities. After six weeks it was clear that Chloe had begun to feel safer and settled in school. She seemed more positive and relaxed, her self-esteem increased and she was gradually becoming less dependent upon adult support. She was able to start taking part in numeracy sessions more confidently and began to make progress and enjoy the activities in the classroom with the rest of her peers.

It is also worth noting that this observation tool and the actions coming from its completion were shared with Chloe's parents at each stage to include them in determining where Chloe's difficulties lay and also in the planning of support offered.

Jacob

The second observation confirms Jacob's escalating difficulties at school. Jacob appears overly reluctant to attend school as he has huge separation anxiety when his carer goes home. In discussion it was felt that his confusion and concern about his home situation overrides his keenness to engage with school staff. He doesn't have a clear idea of who is his primary carer at home; he is therefore unable to make a good secondary secure base with an adult at school, resulting in an overall lack of security.

He therefore finds school and the expectations laid upon him (and some pupils in general) very stressful. It is evident that Jacob is functioning at a much younger age, emotionally.

It is helpful for teachers to notice that often the behaviours displayed by a two- or three-year-old who had been placed in school would be the same as the behaviours children like Jacob exhibit. A two- or three-year-old would quickly become oppositional or belligerent when asked to do something he or she either didn't understand or saw no relevance to. Young children just plainly and simply want to do their own thing, because that's where they are developmentally. When teachers think about how they would support a two- or three-year-old in these circumstances, they can usually suggest the suitable, appropriate strategies for a child like Jacob who is in their class.

Action Plan to Support Observation Checklist

Name of child	Jacob			DOB		Code of Practice
Dates of observation						None SA (SA+) STATEMENT
Involved professionals	Support teacher Educational psychologist					
What works well	Calm, quiet and nurturing Key person role – two staff (in case of staff absence) Boundaries and routine – containment, predictability			Areas for development		Opportunities for sensory needs to be catered for
Concern	**Target**	**How will this be achieved?**		**Resources**		**Who? Where?**
To reduce anxiety-based behaviours in school	For Jacob to come into school and settle down to the school day	Set up a routine for coming into school For carer to ensure a calm journey into school For staff to welcome and 'check-in' with Jacob and carer For staff to direct Jacob and carer to transition activity Prepare Jacob for carer to leave		Calm area Calming activities Transitional objects		Staff Carers School
Concern	**Target**	**How will this be achieved?**		**Resources**		**Who? Where?**
Discipline according to his emotional age/needs	For Jacob to have reduced incidences of dysregulation	For incidences to be recorded and tracked Time in – encourage use of calm area within the classroom Careful transition between activities		Bean bag cushion Calm box Sand timer		Staff School
Concern	**Target**	**How will this be achieved?**		**Resources**		**Who? Where?**
Jacob has difficulty in expressing his feelings appropriately	For Jacob to recognize his feelings and express them appropriately	Protective behaviours programme		Quiet room		Support teacher School
Review date		**Action plan shared with**		Parents Class teacher Teaching assistant SENCO Support teacher Eductional psychologist		

9 Helping the Child with Attachment Difficulties in School

This chapter provides general advice for helping children with attachment difficulties, whatever attachment relationship pattern is being displayed.

Children with attachment difficulties are likely to have more difficulties than the typical child in joining and attending school. These children will have experienced trauma, and/or separation and loss in their early years, involving their primary carers.

School is a source of stress for the child who is likely to be emotionally immature, and not yet ready for the increased independence that attending the school requires. The child may not yet be ready for key challenges of the school environment:

- Tolerating long periods away from their attachment figure.

- Sharing adult support with a group of other children.

- Learning to manage peer relationships, dealing with friendship and conflict.

- Coping with increasing demands for managing routines and the structured environment.

- Developing independence and self-organization.

Standard advice from the English Early Years Foundation Stage implemented in September, 2012 (Department for Education 2012) recommends that:

- Every child is a **unique** child who is constantly learning and can be resilient, capable, confident and self-assured.

- Children will learn to be strong and independent through **positive relationships**.

- Children learn and develop well in **enabling environments**, in which their experiences respond to their individual needs and there is a strong partnership between practitioners and parents or carers.

- Children **develop and learn in different ways**.

Louise Michelle Bombèr (2007), in her book *Inside I'm Hurting*, gives practical strategies for supporting children with attachment difficulties in schools. Louise recommends that children with attachment difficulties who struggle in school will need a carefully chosen key adult to be allocated to them to act as an 'additional attachment figure'. The main part of the role is to develop a relationship with the child, offering the possibility of relative dependency within which the child has the possibility for 'second chance learning'. The role of the key adult can be very powerful in adapting and changing children's interpretation of themselves, others and the world.

Children with attachment difficulties need extra help because they are not yet able to:

- direct attention away from internal needs and focus on tasks
- trust at least one other person
- put feelings into words
- regulate strong negative emotions
- focus attention, sit and concentrate
- feel effective, confident in self
- communicate and cooperate with others
- problem-solve, and resolve conflict
- manage the shame associated with not succeeding
- consistently access learning opportunities.

What do children with attachment difficulties in school need?

Safety

Until children feel safe, they will not be able to derive any positive benefit from being at school. The first priority is therefore to establish a safe environment within which the child can start to feel secure. The child will be helped by a clear structure, boundaries and routine in a relaxing environment and by having opportunities to be in a less stimulating environment. It is important that staff are able to recognize the fear and anxiety that lie beneath behaviour, so that the child can be appropriately supported. Children feel most secure in an environment where the adults set the emotional tone, providing opportunities to co-regulate their escalating arousal. Time and opportunities for rest and relaxation will be important. Staff will also need to recognize the level of support the child needs, especially during times of transition during the school day.

Building a relationship

Children need relationships in order to feel safe, but difficult early relationship experience can make this a difficult need to meet. A key person needs to get to know and understand the child so that he or she can begin the task of engaging the child in the relationship, helping the child to feel safe enough to trust and respond. A teaching assistant can be an effective key person. The class teacher is often not the most appropriate person to fulfil this role, as this teacher also has to manage relationships with all the children in the class (for a detailed discussion of the role of key person, see Bombèr 2007).

The key person will know the child well enough to notice not only the direct but also the distorted requests for help that the child might make. The key person will also be aware of conditions that might throw the child, stepping in early to prevent escalating arousal. This key relationship can then be used to support the child to remain emotionally regulated, and to help the child when feelings of shame or anger threaten to overwhelm him or her. The staff member can also act as advocate or champion for the child within the school, helping other staff to understand the child and to be more fully aware of what the child needs. An attitude of curiosity and reflection will allow staff to stay in tune with the ongoing needs of the child, accepting the feelings that are leading to difficult behaviour and providing empathy and support for complex emotions. Maintaining an attitude of curiosity reduces the likelihood that staff will become angry or critical of the child, helping them to maintain a relationship with the child even at the most difficult moments.

Emotional development

Meeting the emotional needs of children is an important prerequisite for meeting the social and then the learning needs that the child also presents. Children with attachment difficulties are likely to be emotionally immature and to have only fragile control of emotional arousal, whether caused by excitement or anxiety. Staff will need to be attuned to the child so that they can recognize and support feelings however these are displayed, and can step in and provide co-regulation of emotion as required. This co-regulation will be an important part of supporting the child whether or not he or she appears dysregulated. Children who have learnt to inhibit emotion through dissociative processes may also lack these essential regulation skills. While emotional literacy is an important part of education, children will not be able to learn to recognize their own or the feelings of others until they have experienced a sensitive, regulating relationship. Experience of emotional regulation comes before understanding.

Empathy and discipline

Children thrive on structure and boundaries, but this is not sufficient to help them to learn to follow rules and to understand what is acceptable and unacceptable behaviour. This learning arises out of the experience of an empathic, attuned relationship. As children learn to trust in their connection to a nurturing, empathic adult, they also experience shame at the loss of connection when their behaviour meets with disapproval. As the adult comforts and helps the child regulate these feelings of shame, the child is learning what is socially acceptable. Empathy is therefore an important precursor to discipline.

Remember, a child with attachment difficulties is likely to be emotionally young and any use of structure, supervision and discipline needs to take account of this developmental age. Children will need limited and simplified choices and consequences, and help to understand cause and effect.

Clear, calm discipline is important. Behavioural expectations can be provided through explicit rules with predictable and logical consequences for unacceptable behaviour. It is important to provide this in a calm and non-confrontational way. Discipline with empathy and not anger, for example, 'I know it is really hard for you not to take my things when you are angry with me, but remember that you now have to …'

Children with poor cause and effect thinking will need explicit help, much as a parent does with a toddler, to understand the links between their behaviour and the consequence and to understand the impact of themselves on others and others on themselves.

With this approach to discipline it is easier to maintain a positive emotional rhythm within the classroom and to avoid getting pulled into confrontation and anger.

Controlling children can present a particular challenge; entering control battles is rarely successful. Learning to step aside from confrontation and allowing children to experience a safe sense of being in control under the overall supervision of the adults will be helpful to them. From this they will develop trust in the adults. By providing an appropriate time for the child to feel in control, the child will be supported to trust in and enjoy the adult being in charge.

> Meeting emotional needs provides a foundation for social and cognitive development:
> - developing capacity for enjoyment
> - developing social awareness
> - developing reflectivity, the ability to notice and understand experience.

Summary: what do children with attachment difficulties need?

Safety

- Until children feel safe, they will not be able to derive positive benefit from being in the educational environment.

- Establish a safe environment within which the child can start to feel secure.

- Provide clear structure, boundaries and routine in a relaxing environment.

- Recognize the fear and anxiety that lie beneath behaviour so that the child can be appropriately supported.

- Set the emotional tone, providing opportunities to co-regulate the child's escalating arousal.

- Reduce stimulation and provide opportunities for rest and relaxation.

- Support during times of transition during the school day.

Building a relationship

- Children need relationships in order to feel safe.

- A key person gets to know and understand the child and begins engaging the child in the relationship, helping the child to feel safe enough to trust and respond.

- The key person will know the child well enough to notice distorted as well as direct requests for help.

- The key person will be aware of conditions that might throw the child, stepping in early to prevent escalating arousal.

- This key relationship will support emotional regulation, and help the child when feelings of shame or anger threaten to overwhelm.

- The key person can also act as advocate or champion for the child.

- An attitude of curiosity and reflection will allow the key person to stay in tune with the ongoing needs of the child, accepting the feelings that are leading to difficult behaviour and providing empathy and support for complex emotions.

Emotional development

- Need to meet the emotional needs of children when meeting social and learning needs.

- Children with attachment difficulties are likely to be emotionally immature and to have only fragile control of emotional arousal, whether caused by excitement or anxiety.

- Co-regulation is an important part of supporting children whether or not they appear dysregulated.

- Children who have learnt to inhibit emotion through dissociative processes may also lack these essential regulation skills.

- Children will not learn to recognize their own or the feelings of others until they have experienced a sensitive, regulating relationship.

- Experience of emotional regulation comes before understanding.

- Attune to the child to recognize and support feelings however these are displayed.

- Step in and provide co-regulation of emotion as required.

Empathy and discipline

- Empathy is an important precursor to discipline. Discipline with empathy and not anger, e.g. 'I know it is really hard for you not to take my things when you are angry with me, but remember that you now have to ...'

- Learning to follow rules; to understand what is acceptable and unacceptable behaviour arises out of the experience of an empathic, attuned relationship.

- As the adult comforts and helps the child regulate the feelings of shame, the child is learning what is socially acceptable.

- Children with attachment difficulties are likely to be emotionally young.

- Children will need limited and simplified choices and consequences, and help to understand cause and effect.

- Provide explicit rules with predictable and logical consequences for unacceptable behaviour in a calm and non-confrontational way.

- Support understanding of behaviour and its consequences and the impact of themselves on others and others on themselves.

- Avoid getting pulled into confrontation and anger.

- By providing an appropriate time for the child to feel in control the child will be supported to trust in and enjoy the adult being in charge.

How can we meet these needs in school?

(For further detail about meeting emotional needs, and especially the role of the key adult the reader is referred to Louise Michelle Bombèr (2007, 2011).)

All children, whatever attachment pattern they display, will benefit from the following:

- Use activities that involve relationship-based play. Relationship-based play is modelled on healthy parent–infant relationships. The focus of the play is the relationship. It is playful, interactive and empathic. In this type of play, the main task is enjoying being together. This is different from more task-focused play when, for example, you help the child to complete a puzzle or to learn colours. Relationship-based play makes minimal use of materials but lots of use of the relationship between the adult and the child. This type of play can be adapted for children of all ages.

- Help to regulate high levels of excitement, anger or anxiety. 'Time in' rather than 'time out' can be used to provide the child with time away from activities and time with a supportive adult. In particular, following difficult behaviour, the adult sits with the child and helps him or her with the feelings that underlie the behaviour.

- Help to feel safe in school, with special attention to times of transition, changes of routine and when visitors attend the classroom.

- Ensure predictable and consistent routines and structure. When these routines and structures have to be disrupted because of planned or unplanned events, the child is likely to need time to adjust to the change. Simple explanations sometimes accompanied with a visual cue to remind the child about the change and more attention to supporting the child during the change can be helpful.

- Think younger. Children who need a high level of emotional support tend to be emotionally immature, even if they are generally bright with a good ability to learn. These children often struggle with expectations typical for their age group but respond well when expectations are adjusted to a younger emotional age, and additional support is provided.

- As a rule of thumb, an 'emotionally healthy' five-year-old can concentrate happily for five minutes at a time, a seven-year-old for 15 minutes at a time and an eleven-year-old for 20 minutes.

Allocation and role of a key person

One of the ways in which these benefits can be provided is by allocating a key person.

Creating a secure base

The key person can ensure that a secure base is created for the child.

- The key person is an active presence, not an observer. This role is an important tool in the child's social and emotional education.

- The key person and the child need time to spend together, to connect and begin to build a relationship. This ensures that the key person is tuned in and available to the child.

- The key person will initiate and supervise games, activities and conversations between the child and his or her peers, supporting the development of social skills and friendships.

- The key person's aim is to become a secondary attachment figure for the child, while he or she is away from the primary attachment figures.

- The key person helps the child to learn to become dependent, a necessary developmental stage before he or she is able to become an independent learner.

The key person will provide consistency and be able to recognize triggers and signals that indicate that the child is beginning to struggle with his or her emotions.

Providing emotional support

The key person can ensure that emotional support is provided for the child.

- Give the child the experience of feeling safe and lovable. All children deserve love and affection regardless of their ability to conform.

- Support and build relationships with the child at the emotional age he or she is displaying rather than the chronological age.

- Set the emotional tone for the child. The adult stays calm and nurturing, especially at times when the child is becoming dysregulated. Staying calm does not necessarily mean being quiet; an intense but calm tone which matches the intensity of the child's feelings will more quickly help the child to regulate. This is called affect matching. The adult matches the vitality and intensity of the expression of emotion by the child. If the child is sad, the adult will be quieter and softer. If the child is angry, adults need to be more intense in tone without becoming angry themselves.

- Acknowledge, reassure and provide security for a child in a physical, verbal or feelings-based way (emotional containment).

- Provide a calm area in the school for rest and relaxation when anxiety levels seem to be rising.

- Provide a calm box with sensory toys and activities when anxiety levels seem to be rising.

- Tune in to the child's behaviour in the context of the underlying emotion.

- Pay attention to interactive or relationship repair, re-establishing a positive relationship with the child following a disruption to this relationship.

- Allow processing time between chunks of information.

- Be prepared to repeat, repeat, repeat: 1. The child hears. 2. The child absorbs information. 3. The child acts.

Providing behavioural support

The key person can ensure that behavioural support is provided for the child.

- Reflect on the possible underlying causes of a child's non-compliance. This may be a signal that the child feels anxious, perhaps fearful of change or endings. These feelings need supporting.

- Choose the battles. Ignore, pre-empt, redirect and distract, as you would for a younger child.

- Plan ahead. Think about what you will do when an outburst occurs. Practise what strategies you will use, such as taking the child to a calm area with sensory activities.

- Be clear while being supportive and empathic. Use a warm, matter-of-fact tone.

- Try not to confront, as this can lead to an increase in anxiety and can escalate behaviour.

- Think about the effect of 'time out' on a child who has already experienced rejection.

- Use 'time in' to calm the child and reduce his or her anxiety.

- Think about the effect of stickers and rewards on a child who doesn't believe him or herself deserving of love and treats. Short, descriptive praise and rewards for very specific behaviours (e.g. 'You shared your pencils very nicely with X') might be easier for the child to accept than more global praise and rewards (e.g. 'You have been very good today').

- Wonder aloud to make sense of behaviour (e.g. 'I think you might be feeling a bit angry because it is time to tidy up...'). Use sentences such as 'I know this is hard for you ...'; 'I am wondering if you are feeling...'; 'I guess you are really feeling ...'.

Providing learning support

The key person can ensure that learning support is provided for the child.

- Prepare the child for any change in routine in advance. Change can be scary.

- Routines and boundaries are important to help a child feel safe, but not too rigid. Be flexible and adapt to the child's needs.

- Help the child to remember that he or she is being 'kept in mind' by his or her parent throughout the day, to reduce feelings of abandonment.

- Model and initiate play skills, and good social interactions with peers and adults.

- Provide explicit teaching of playground protocols and games.

- You may need to give the child short periods to practise independence.

- Give consistent, clear and simple instructions.

- Use a visual timetable to reinforce instructions. This can help the child to understand what is going to happen next when he or she is too anxious to hear properly or understand.

- Look for opportunities to build self-esteem. It is important for children to feel good about themselves. Celebrate success and good choices. For example, use photographs to reinforce and evidence these. These can be shared with the child regularly.

Looking after the key person

The key person can ensure that they look after themselves.

- Talk to colleagues and seek support. This is hard work!

- Be prepared for the long haul. Change takes time.

- Make good use of supervision and opportunities to reflect with others about the child.

- Notice small signs of progress, and hold on to these during the more difficult times.

- Try not to take behaviours directed towards you personally. Remember, the child does not know how to manage angry feelings. Children tend to target those they feel safest with when they have feelings they can't otherwise manage.

- Have a back-up key person to support you. This person will also need to develop a relationship with the child.

Summary: the role of the key person

Creating a secure base

- The key person as an active presence.

- Helping the child to become dependent before becoming independent.

- Tune in (attunement) and be available.

- Develop capacity for enjoyment.

- Let the child know he or she is being kept in mind (mind-mindedness).

- Initiate and supervise games, activities and conversations between the child and his or her peers.

Providing emotional support

- Acknowledge, reassure and provide security in a physical, verbal or feelings-based way (emotional containment).

- Set the emotional tone (affect matching).

- Provide relationship repair following times of rupture.

- Give the child the experience of feeling safe and lovable.

- Provide a calm area for rest and relaxation.

- Provide a calm box with sensory toys and activities.

- Support and build relationships with the child at the emotional age he or she is displaying.

Providing behavioural support

- Avoid confrontation.

- Reflect on the possible underlying cause.

- Be clear, while being supportive and empathic.

- Use 'time in' rather than time out.

- Ignore, pre-empt, redirect and distract.

- Wonder aloud.

- Don't take projections personally.

Providing learning support

- Provide predictable and consistent routines and structure.

- Prepare the child for any change in routine in advance.

- Provide boundaries to help a child feel safe.

- Be flexible and adapt to the child's needs.

- Give the child short periods to practise independence.

- Give consistent, clear and simple instructions.

- Use a visual timetable to reinforce instructions.

- Look for opportunities to build self-esteem.

- Celebrate success and good choices, e.g. photographs.

The importance of support

Supporting a child with attachment difficulties is hard work. It is therefore important that adults are well supported. Time for reflection is important – to be able to step back from the situation and think with others about what is going on for the child, and understand the relationship that is developing.

Networks and multi-agency working

Children with attachment difficulties can have complex networks built up around them. Good communication and working together within these networks is an important part of supporting the child. By working together, professionals will develop a shared understanding about the child and what the child needs. It is also an important part of avoiding splitting within the network. Children with attachment difficulties can have very concrete and immature thinking abilities; finding it difficult to hold on to different perspectives, they view others and experiences as 'all good' or 'all bad'. Without good multi-agency working, networks get pulled in to these immature thinking processes so that parts of the network become the all-good rescuers while other parts become the all-bad persecutors.

Support for the adults

The staff working directly with the child with an attachment difficulty will need good support, training and opportunities for high quality supervision which facilitates reflection and planning.

The risks of secondary trauma when working with traumatized children are high (Cairns and Stanway 2004). Good supervision can ensure that early signs of secondary trauma are noticed and appropriate and timely support provided.

The key person will become a transitional attachment figure to the child, but will need to avoid the child forming a secondary attachment to the adult which is at the expense of the primary attachment to the carer. Helping the child know that his or her parent or carer is thinking about him or her during the school day, and receiving from and handing back to the primary attachment figure at the beginning and end of the day is an important part of the support that is provided.

We have all encountered a range of relationships in the past – some rewarding and some more difficult. Working with a child with attachment difficulties can remind staff of their own early attachment experience, interfering with their ability to relate to the child in the present and to experience empathy for the child. In working with children with attachment difficulties, it is therefore important that staff have a good understanding of their own attachment and past relationship experience. This will then allow them to stay truly in the present with the child in front of them.

Conclusion

Secure attachment gives the child the opportunity to feel safe, to trust, to relate, to be dependent and to be independent. The child with attachment difficulties has not had this experience. These children bring their fear, their lack of trust, their difficulties with relationships, their unfulfilled dependency needs and their struggles with independence into school. We need to provide school environments within which we can help the child to feel safe and secure – meeting his or her emotional needs and providing the foundation for learning. The starting point for this is close working together leading to a shared understanding of the child and what the child needs.

10

Helping the Child with Different Attachment Styles in School

Following on from Chapter 9, which provided a general exploration of how schools can meet the attachment needs of children with emotional difficulties, this chapter provides more specific advice for helping children in relation to the different attachment patterns of relating that they might display. Not all children fit neatly into these patterns, but may show combinations of these styles. In this case combinations of the tailored advice might be helpful.

Helping the child with insecure avoidant patterns of relating within the school setting

Children with insecure avoidant patterns of relating tend towards being self-reliant within the classroom. They experience difficulty seeking or using help from adults. Thus when the child feels insecure or in need of assistance he or she is reluctant to seek this support. The goal of the teacher is to help the child feel more secure within the school so that he or she is more confident in using the support on offer. The child can be helped in achieving this goal by providing a high level of structure and routine. Geddes (2006) suggests that the task can provide needed structure which then helps the child to experience safety in the relationship with the adults. These children may find it easier to be in a small group, this can help them cope with proximity to the adult. Additionally older children can be buddies for younger children.

Children with avoidant styles of relating benefit from having some choice in the content of the activity. The adults gradually help children to build their confidence in seeking and using help. It is helpful to let the child experience being thought about and held in mind, for example, 'I thought about you this weekend when ...'.

> ## Helping the child with an insecure avoidant attachment
>
> These children tend to miscue the adults regarding their need for nurturing. When they need emotional closeness, they act as if they don't need the adult. Help the avoidant child by taking care of hurts, however minor.
>
> Find opportunities to nurture them and encourage them to accept reassurance when distressed. These children need help to focus on and express their feelings. They also need help to feel good about themselves and to cope with not being the best, and sometimes getting things wrong.

Helping the child who withdraws

Some children will dissociate when stressed. This is a cutting off from emotion. These children may display little emotion or may move quickly from one emotion to another. This makes it difficult to feel emotionally connected to them. These children need help to stay with their feelings. Reflect back feelings that they may be experiencing, for example, 'If I were you I would be feeling really angry right now'. If they are very 'switched off', try to encourage them 'back to the present'. Remind them of who they are, where they are and who you are.

Figure 10.1 provides a visual summary of the behaviours that children display as part of the avoidant attachment pattern, and interventions that might be helpful for them.

Summary: insecure avoidant attachment pattern of relating

Insecure avoidant profile	Interventions
Attachment pattern develops out of a relationship with a parent who is distant and rejecting These children need help to focus on and express their feelings	
• Withdrawn and quiet • Rely on knowledge and ignore feelings to guide behaviours • Generally appear more self-reliant and independent than expected for their age • Reluctant to turn to adults when they need help • Distress is denied or not communicated • May try to take care of the teacher • Can appear happy or settled much of the time • If stressed, may show a sudden and apparently inexplicable tantrum which is quickly over • Relatively isolated as they lack emotional engagement with other children or with adults • Avoid intimacy • May appear more focused on activities than on people • Resistant to help from the teacher but also lack confidence in their own ability • Focus more on what they can't do rather than what they can do • Fear of failure • Act with indifference to new situations	• Find opportunities to nurture • Encourage accepting the adult taking care of hurts, however minor • Help to feel good about themselves and to cope with not being the best, and sometimes getting things wrong • Organise small groups as the child may find this easier • Support in coping with the proximity of the adult • Arrange for older children to be buddies for younger children • Allow some choice in content of play and activities • Gradually build child's ability to accept help • Help the child to experience being thought about and held in mind. *'I thought about you this weekend when …'* • Structure games with clear rules • Plan clear, structured tasks with all your materials to hand • Use questions, which are factual and precise • Use sorting objects and building structures

Insecure avoidant profile	Interventions
• Can show limited use of creativity and imagination • Likely to be underachievers • Limited use of language	• Use TV, films and videos to help describe characters' emotions • Give concrete structured activities • If possible use the pupil's own experience rather than abstract • Use 'writing frames' – filling in boxes, completing sentences and writing brief sentences in defined spaces can help with the anxiety of 'spilling out' onto a blank page • Plan activities involving swinging, rolling, spinning – these can be extremely helpful in helping to increase low arousal • Initially avoid games that are about winning and losing but focus on games that are simply about having fun
Expressed need	Hidden need
I will do it by myself. I fear my need of you. I will push you away	I will not show my need for comfort and protection

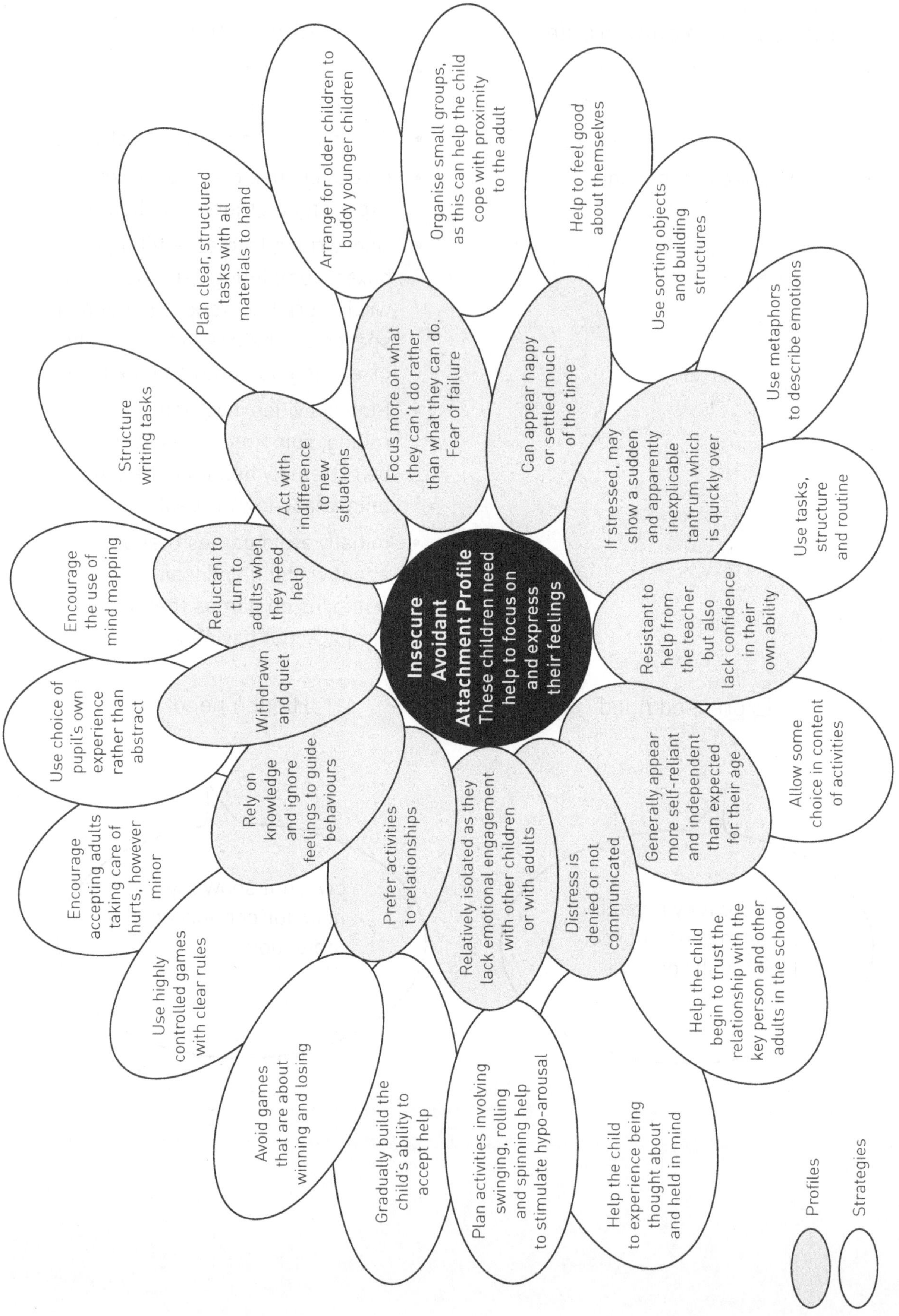

Center (Profile):
Insecure Avoidant Attachment Profile These children need help to focus on and express their feelings

Profiles (shaded petals):
- Act with indifference to new situations
- Focus more on what they can't do rather than what they can do. Fear of failure
- Can appear happy or settled much of the time
- If stressed, may show a sudden and apparently inexplicable tantrum which is quickly over
- Reluctant to turn to adults when they need help
- Resistant to help from the teacher but also lack confidence in their own ability
- Withdrawn and quiet
- Rely on knowledge and ignore feelings to guide behaviours
- Generally appear more self-reliant and independent than expected for their age
- Prefer activities to relationships
- Relatively isolated as they lack emotional engagement with other children or with adults
- Distress is denied or not communicated

Strategies (white petals):
- Plan clear, structured tasks with all materials to hand
- Arrange for older children to buddy younger children
- Organise small groups, as this can help the child cope with proximity to the adult
- Help to feel good about themselves
- Use sorting objects and building structures
- Use metaphors to describe emotions
- Use tasks, structure and routine
- Allow some choice in content of activities
- Help the child begin to trust the relationship with the key person and other adults in the school
- Help the child to experience being thought about and held in mind
- Plan activities involving swinging, rolling and spinning help to stimulate hypo-arousal
- Gradually build the child's ability to accept help
- Avoid games that are about winning and losing
- Use highly controlled games with clear rules
- Encourage accepting adults taking care of hurts, however minor
- Use choice of pupil's own experience rather than abstract
- Encourage the use of mind mapping
- Structure writing tasks

Legend:
- Profiles
- Strategies

FIGURE 10.1 INSECURE AVOIDANT ATTACHMENT PROFILE

Helping the child with insecure ambivalent patterns of relating within school

Children with insecure ambivalent patterns of relating tend towards being attention-needing and clingy. It is difficult for these children to focus on the activity because all their focus is on checking out the availability of the adults. They quickly feel anxious when they experience a degree of separation and therefore behave in ways which restores the connection with the adult again. The goal is to help the children feel confident enough in the availability of the adult that they can reduce their focus on this in order to attend to the activity. The adults can be helped in reaching this goal by providing highly predictable, structured routines and visual timetables to help the children to follow the routines. Turn-taking with the adult can help the child achieve some independence in activities.

Geddes (2006) recommends differentiating tasks into small independent steps and using a timer to help the child cope with brief independent times away from the adult. Additionally transitional objects (looking after something for the adult) can help a child to cope with times apart. The child needs to experience being noticed by the adults frequently during the day. They can use comments to let the child know that they are thinking about him or her. Special attention needs to be given to transition times when these children feel particularly anxious.

These children are helped if the adults provide reliable and consistent support, facilitating a gradually increasing separation and attention to activities. It is important not to reduce these supports too quickly; allow the child to develop more independence slowly.

> ### Helping the child with an insecure ambivalent attachment
>
> These children tend to miscue the adults about their need for attention. They will be reluctant to signal that they don't need you close at the moment because they will fear that you might not be close when they do need you.
>
> These children need lots of attention, support and nurturing while also being encouraged to cope with short periods without your constant attention. These periods can then be gradually extended. These children need help to understand behaviour and its predictable consequences ('When I do this, this happens; when you do this, this happens'). They also need help to regulate strong emotions. Support them in calming down so that they can learn how to calm themselves down.

Figure 10.2 provides a visual summary of the behaviours that children display as part of the ambivalent attachment pattern, and interventions that might be helpful for them.

Summary: insecure ambivalent attachment pattern of relating

Insecure ambivalent profile	Interventions
Attachment pattern develops out of a relationship with a parent who is inconsistent and unpredictable The children need lots of attention, support and nurturing while also being encouraged to cope with short periods without your constant attention	
• Tend to make their presence known • Preoccupied with relationships, alert to the availability of others • Appear attention-needing, highly dependent • Overly focused on the relationship with the teacher or teaching assistant at the expense of learning • Find it difficult to settle by themselves or with groups of children • Sometimes talk excessively, or act as 'class clown' in order to maintain the focus of adult attention • Concentrating and focusing on tasks is difficult as they remain hypervigilant to what the adults are doing and are easily distracted • Very focused on feelings • Find it difficult to attend to the rules and structure of the classroom • Find it difficult to follow rules and to learn from consequences • Poor understanding of cause and effect. Find it difficult to take responsibility for behaviour and learning • Rely on feelings rather than knowledge to guide their behaviour	• Provide highly predictable, structured routines • Use visual timetables • Differentiate tasks into small steps • Encourage turn-taking to help achieve some independence in activities • Use a sand timer to help calm anxieties during short timed independent tasks • Provide special transitional objects to take place of teacher for a short while. *'Please look after this for me for a while'* • Notice the child frequently during the day. Use comments to let child know you are thinking about him or her • Provide reliable and consistent adult support • Gradually increase separation • Don't reduce these supports too quickly • Allow the child to develop more independence slowly • Use stories around issues of separation, identity and independence • Encourage responsibility for tasks

Insecure ambivalent profile	Interventions
• Keep others involved in relationships through coercive behaviours. Seen as manipulative • Can escalate confrontation in order to hold the attention of others • View the teacher as either all good or all bad, and may oscillate between these depending on their immediate feeling • Find it hard to maintain friendships and can be clingy and possessive • Oversensitive to signs of rejection	• Support understanding of their behaviour and the predictable consequences. *'When I do this, this happens; when you do this, this happens'* • Pay special attention to transition times • Plan beginnings, separations, endings • Support the anxiety of the unknown • Support them in regulating strong emotions and in calming down so that they can learn how to calm themselves down • Give 'permission' cards – these can be used by child to 'bank' if the teacher is busy and can't give the child attention immediately. The child can use them to 'book' a prearranged time later on • Plan calming and regulating activities involving physical resistance and deep pressure touch to help ground them
Expressed need	Hidden need
I can't trust in your availability. I need you to attend to me	I will not show my need to separate and explore. I will pull you in and push you away

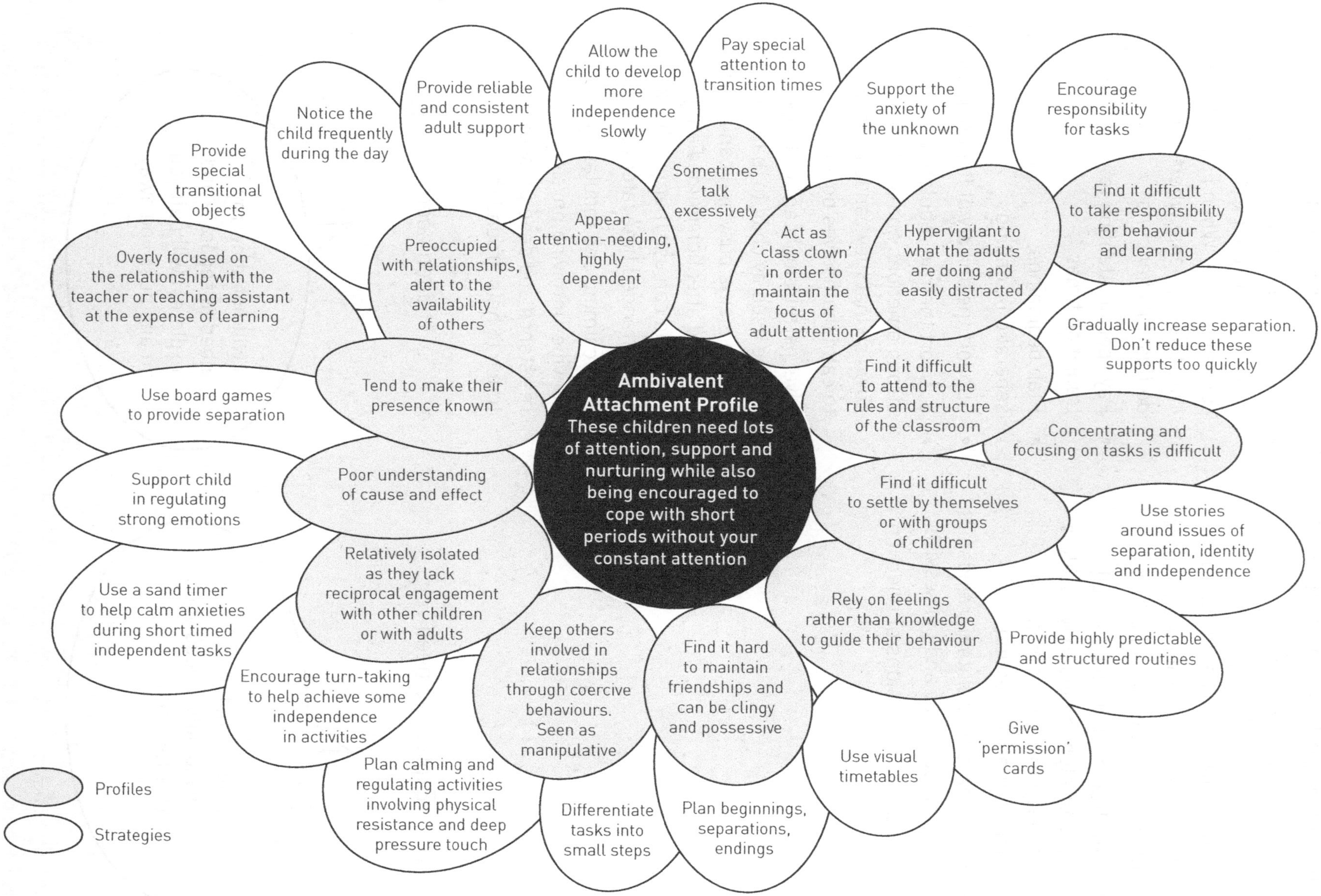

Ambivalent Attachment Profile
These children need lots of attention, support and nurturing while also being encouraged to cope with short periods without your constant attention

Profiles:
- Find it difficult to take responsibility for behaviour and learning
- Concentrating and focusing on tasks is difficult
- Hypervigilant to what the adults are doing and easily distracted
- Find it difficult to attend to the rules and structure of the classroom
- Find it difficult to settle by themselves or with groups of children
- Rely on feelings rather than knowledge to guide their behaviour
- Act as 'class clown' in order to maintain the focus of adult attention
- Find it hard to maintain friendships and can be clingy and possessive
- Sometimes talk excessively
- Appear attention-needing, highly dependent
- Keep others involved in relationships through coercive behaviours. Seen as manipulative
- Preoccupied with relationships, alert to the availability of others
- Tend to make their presence known
- Poor understanding of cause and effect
- Relatively isolated as they lack reciprocal engagement with other children or with adults

Strategies:
- Encourage responsibility for tasks
- Gradually increase separation. Don't reduce these supports too quickly
- Use stories around issues of separation, identity and independence
- Provide highly predictable and structured routines
- Give 'permission' cards
- Support the anxiety of the unknown
- Use visual timetables
- Pay special attention to transition times
- Plan beginnings, separations, endings
- Allow the child to develop more independence slowly
- Differentiate tasks into small steps
- Provide reliable and consistent adult support
- Plan calming and regulating activities involving physical resistance and deep pressure touch
- Notice the child frequently during the day
- Encourage turn-taking to help achieve some independence in activities
- Provide special transitional objects
- Overly focused on the relationship with the teacher or teaching assistant at the expense of learning
- Use board games to provide separation
- Support child in regulating strong emotions
- Use a sand timer to help calm anxieties during short timed independent tasks

Profiles
Strategies

FIGURE 10.2 INSECURE AMBIVALENT ATTACHMENT PATTERN PROFILE

Disciplining the child with insecure attachment

Clear, calm discipline is important. Behavioural expectations can be provided through explicit rules with predictable and logical consequences for unacceptable behaviour. It is important to provide this in a calm and non-confrontational way. Discipline with empathy and not anger (e.g. 'I know it is really hard for you not to take my things when you are angry with me, but remember that you now have to …').

Children with poor cause and effect thinking will need explicit help, much as a parent does with a toddler, to understand the links between their behaviour and the consequence and to understand the impact of themselves on others and others on themselves.

With this approach to discipline, it is easier to maintain a positive emotional rhythm within the setting and to avoid getting pulled into confrontation and anger.

Helping the child with disorganized-controlling patterns of relating within school

Children with disorganized-controlling patterns of relating feel highly unsafe and tend towards being angry, aggressive and highly controlling with the adults and the other children. It is difficult for these children to focus on the activity or on the availability of the adult because all their focus is on checking out and trying to ensure their safety. They quickly feel anxious when they experience any unpredictability, uncertainty or the unexpected, and work hard to force the environment to be predictable again. The goal for the adults is to help the child feel safe within the school. These children have very poor stress tolerance and therefore stress needs to be kept to a minimum while they slowly build up their ability to manage stress. The adults can be helped in reaching this goal by providing highly safe and predictable environments, reducing the unexpected or the unplanned to a minimum. Adults need to help the child to feel physically safe and contained by providing high levels of calm non-confrontational responses, empathy, and understanding to help the child feel emotionally contained. Be aware of the emotional level the child is functioning at; provide activities and experiences matched to this level. Adults can develop safety routines and plans to be engaged when the child is very distressed. Think about the place (quiet, non-stimulating) and provide time with the key person.

Geddes (2006) suggests that concrete, mechanical and rhythmic activities can help soothe an over-aroused child, for example, matching, colouring, sand, water and sensory play. Rhythmical physical exercise and music can also help an aroused child calm down. Older children can have a permission card to use when they need to go to a safe place without need for explanation.

Helping the child with a controlling pattern of relating

When children are displaying a lot of controlling, manipulative and aggressive behaviour or overly compliant and withdrawn behaviour, they are signalling that they are feeling anxious, distressed and insecure.

They will need a period of reduced stress and high security. This includes reducing excitement and providing calm, predictable and low-key routine. As they relax they will be open to accepting care and support, leading to a reduction of the controlling behaviours.

Figure 10.3 provides a visual summary of the behaviours that children display as part of the disorganized-controlling attachment pattern, and interventions that might be helpful for them.

Summary: disorganized-controlling attachment pattern of relating

Disorganized-controlling profile	Interventions
Attachment pattern develops out of a relationship within which the parent is frightened of or frightening to the child When children are displaying a lot of controlling, manipulative and aggressive behaviour or overly compliant and withdrawn behaviour, they are signalling that they are feeling anxious, distressed and insecure	
<ul><li>May be either quiet and withdrawn or loud and aggressive</li><li>Controlling within peer relationships. May want friendships but immaturity impedes this</li><li>Anxiety may be expressed as controlling, omnipotent, knowing everything already</li><li>Demonstrate a diminished range of emotions, lacking the contentment and joy in activities of other children</li><li>Frequently afraid but tend to mask anxiety through more aggressive or powerful behaviours. May provoke, bully or challenge others to maintain feelings of control</li><li>May have poor stress tolerance, detracts from learning</li><li>Can be highly disruptive in school</li><li>Tend to be anxious and inattentive</li><li>May demonstrate highly compulsive or obsessive behaviours which allow them to hold on to a rigid control</li><li>May appear compliant but resist attempts to be helped or comforted</li><li>Some children portray a pseudomature care-giving role within the classroom</li><li>Others may demonstrate more obsessive preoccupations with being noticed through a combination of aggressive and coy behaviours</li></ul>	<ul><li>Provide a period of reduced stress and high security</li><li>Reduce excitement and providing calm, predictable and low-key routine</li><li>Provide highly safe and secure environments with reliable and predictable routines which helps reduce stress</li><li>Help the child to feel physically safe and contained</li><li>Use calm non-confrontational responses, empathy</li><li>Help the child feel emotionally contained. A 'safe' area/ activity/object helps with this</li><li>Be aware of the emotional, social and developmental level the child is functioning at and provide activities and experiences that match to this</li><li>Plan concrete, mechanical and rhythmic activities to help soothe an over-aroused child, e.g. matching, colouring, sand and water play, sensory play</li><li>Use rhythmical physical exercise and music to help an aroused child calm down</li></ul>

Disorganized-controlling profile	Interventions
• Hypervigilant to what is going on around them, making it difficult to concentrate or attend to a task • Their early brain development has developed over-responsive fight-or-flight reactions, leaving a diminished capacity to concentrate or think • Although hyper-aroused, some cope with excessive feelings of stress by dissociating – appearing 'switched-off' • Strong feelings are overwhelming • May find it hard to understand, distinguish or control emotions in themselves or others • Immaturity and rigid controlling style of relating to other children can lead to social isolation • Likely to be underachieves and possibly at a very immature stage of learning • May be unable to accept being taught, and/or are threatened by others knowing more than they do as this triggers overwhelming feelings of humiliation • Struggle in relatively unsupervised settings such as the playground or moving between lessons	• Develop safety and or calming routines for when the child is very distressed. *Think about the place (quiet, non-stimulating) and provide time with the key person* • Wherever possible, give positive comments about achievement, whether about behaviour or in terms of task • Try to address the class/group generally rather than directly to pupil • Depending on concentration span – engage in short task interspersed with mechanical tasks, e.g. computer or 'safe' activity in order to calm the brain • Give 'permission' cards – these can be used by child to 'bank' if the teacher is busy and can't give the child attention immediately. Child can use them to 'book' a prearranged time later on
Expressed need	Hidden need
I will not need you. Needing you is dangerous. I must be in control	I can't explore the world. I am too busy ensuring I am safe

Disorganized-Controlling Attachment Profile
When children are displaying a lot of controlling, manipulative and aggressive behaviour or overly compliant and withdrawn behaviour, they are signalling that they are feeling anxious, distressed and insecure

Profiles:

- Strong feelings are overwhelming
- Hypervigilant to what is going on around them, making it difficult to concentrate or attend to a task
- Be aware of the emotional, social and developmental level the child is functioning at and provide activities and experiences that match to this
- Tend to be anxious and inattentive
- May portray a pseudomature care-giving role
- Likely to be underachievers and possibly at a very immature stage of learning
- May demonstrate highly compulsive or obsessive behaviours which allow them to hold on to a rigid control
- May demonstrate more obsessive preoccupations with being noticed through a combination of aggressive and coy behaviours
- Although often hyper-aroused, some cope with excessive feelings of stress by dissociating – appearing 'switched-off'
- Struggle in relatively unsupervised settings such as the playground or moving between lessons
- May appear compliant but resist attempts to be helped or comforted
- May have poor stress tolerance which detracts from learning
- Frequently afraid but tend to mask anxiety through more aggressive or powerful behaviours
- Can be highly disruptive in school
- May provoke, bully or challenge others to maintain feelings of being in control
- Demonstrate a diminished range of emotions
- Controlling within peer relationships leading to a lack of friendships
- May be either quiet and withdrawn or loud and aggressive
- Anxiety may be expressed as controlling, omnipotent and knowing everything already
- May be unable to accept being taught, and/or are threatened by others knowing more than them as this triggers overwhelming feelings of humiliation
- Their immaturity and rigid controlling style of relating to other children can lead to social isolation

Strategies:

- Organise concrete, mechanical and rhythmic activities help soothe an over-aroused child
- Engage in short activities interspersed with mechanical tasks
- Help the child feel emotionally contained
- Ensure the child has a period of reduced stress and high security
- Try to address the class/group generally rather than directly to pupil
- Give positive comments about achievement
- Help the child to feel physically safe and contained
- Create a 'safe' area/activity/object
- Use rhythmical physical exercise and music to help an aroused child calm down
- Give 'permission' cards
- Use calm non-confrontational responses and empathy
- Develop safety and/or calming routines for when the child is very distressed
- Provide highly safe and secure environments with reliable and predictable routines which help to reduce stress
- Reduce excitement and provide calm, predictable and low-key routine

Profiles ⬭
Strategies ⬭

FIGURE 10.3 DISORGANIZED-CONTROLLING ATTACHMENT PROFILE

11 Supporting the Emotional Needs of Children with Attachment Difficulties

Generally there are two aspects to providing support that staff need to consider when individualizing support tailored to a child's emotional needs. First, there will be a range of support already present which could be helpful for the child, but staff need to find ways to help the child access this support. For example, regular outside play can help a child who struggles with focus and concentration. The more active play can help the child to relax and release some tension. The child might have difficulties making the transition from indoors to outdoors, however, or may struggle to use this relatively unstructured time. A key adult will need to provide some additional support to help the child make best use of this activity.

This can be challenging because the child with attachment difficulties has a basic distrust of adults. The child needs to be helped to build up security with a trusted adult, who can then help the child to use the support on offer.

Second, children may benefit from some innovative practice tailored to their needs. This will place more demands on staff but can be highly effective for some children. Again supporting the child to access this support will be key to its success.

For example, a child might be displaying excessive attention neediness from the key adult. This might make it very difficult for this child to cope with the gentle challenge of managing an activity without this close attention, or coping when the adult takes a break. The use of a transitional object, holding on to something that belongs to the adult, might be a way to help the child 'hold on' to that adult in his or her absence.

Challenges in supporting the emotional needs of children with attachment difficulties

There are a range of challenges which can face staff when they try to develop a plan for supporting an individual child, as described below.

Managing need for dependency versus independence

One important aspect of school life relies on children having some degree of independence. They will be most successful if they can manage without a parent figure around and if they become increasingly independent as they progress through the school. When a child's identified needs are for increased dependency, this can seem at odds with a key objective for the child. Staff might be tempted to push the child to be more independent, believing that this will serve him or her better in the future. This can be unhelpful. The route to independence is via dependency. It can be a mistake to try to move children too quickly to more independent activities when they are not yet ready for it. Understanding the emotional age of the child and gearing support to this emotional age is a key part of supporting the emotional needs of the child with attachment difficulties.

This can be a double challenge when supporting children who have learnt to deal with their emotional distress through self-reliance. An apparent 'pseudomaturity', appearing more mature than they actually are, can mask the dependency needs of some children. Staff need to hold on to an assessment that a child needs to be more dependent, and to support the child to accept dependency when he or she distrusts reliance on others. This can be additionally challenging when it appears counter to the objective of the school to help children be more independent.

Maintaining high boundaries and high warmth

Research has shown that all children do best in an atmosphere of authoritative parenting (Hetherington and Parke 1993). This is parenting that provides a high degree of warmth while both encouraging autonomy and providing clear and consistent boundaries. Children with attachment difficulties need and thrive best on this same combination of autonomy, boundaries and warmth in schools. The boundaries provide consistency, predictability, routines and clear consequences. The encouragement of autonomy, but matched to the child's capacity, provides the gentle challenge that moves the child forward and the warmth provides nurturing support.

Maintaining high warmth can be difficult. For example, starting with empathy and concern for a child can feel like being soft, or giving in to him or her. If children are to benefit from consequences and behavioural guidance they will need support for their emotional insecurity. This is what the warmth and nurture provides. Children with attachment difficulties often have a core belief in their own badness. Without a high degree of warmth from supportive adults, they are much more likely to enter a state of shame. Experience of shame tends to further cut children off from the relationships that they most need while reinforcing the maladaptive relationship strategies that are maintaining their insecurity and emotional distress.

Managing behaviour while supporting emotional development

A school is a social environment with its own set of expectations and values. We want the children within the school to conform to these. The challenging behaviour of the child with complex emotional needs can oppose our expectations and values. The usual response to such behaviours is to discourage these behaviours and encourage alternative behaviours. This is the basis of behavioural management programmes. We use rewards and consequences to help the other come in line with our expectations. Thus we reward a behaviour we want to increase and provide a negative consequence for a behaviour we want to reduce. In this way we provide a 'correction' for the behaviour. While this might be an effective way to manage behaviour, it is not a helpful way to influence emotional development. Emotional development thrives on connection not correction. In other words, when we connect emotionally to a child, recognizing and understanding the emotional experience which has led to the behaviour, we are also helping that child to develop emotionally. Children need both connection and correction. Children with attachment difficulties are at particular risk of missing out on connection. This is because their difficulties make them distrustful of emotional connection with another and because the behaviours can be especially difficult leading to a focus on these rather than on the emotional experience of the child. When developing support tailored to the emotional needs of the child, it is vital that attention is given to how the adults can emotionally connect to the child before they manage the behaviour that the child is presenting, that is, connection before correction.

Supporting children with shame-based difficulties

Many children with attachment difficulties will struggle with the experience of shame. The development of shame is influenced by the early relationship experience of the child. The experience of shame emerges at a time in the child's development when he or she is becoming more mobile. It is part of the socialization process. When parents tell their children 'no' or discourage them from particular behaviours, the attunement experienced by the children with their parents is temporarily disrupted. This break in attunement is experienced as a sense of shame, therefore discouraging the behaviour the child was engaged in. Sensitive parents will then 'repair the relationship'; re-establishing attunement with the children by letting them know that they are still loved, any disapproval of the behaviour does not affect the relationship the parent has with the children.

When children experience little attunement with parents; when discipline is harsh, punitive or inconsistent and when parents do not attend to relationship repair, children will experience overwhelming and unregulated shame. This experience of shame becomes tied up with the child's developing sense of identity. The child no longer experiences him or herself as having done a 'bad thing' but as being a 'bad person'. Instead of the healthy development of guilt, an emotion which drives us to make amends, to connect with the person wronged and put it right; the child gets stuck in shame. This emotion leads to a desire to hide away from other people, preventing the ability to make amends.

Children bring this early experience of shame and guilt into the classroom. Healthy development means that children can take responsibility for their behaviour, experiencing guilt and being able to make amends, with the support of the teacher or teaching assistant. Children with shame-based difficulties react more defensively. They cannot respond to the other because they are too busy defending against the feelings of shame in themselves. They put up a 'shield against the shame': they lie, minimize, blame others or when all else fails they rage (see Figure 11.1).

FIGURE 11.1 SHIELD AGAINST SHAME (FROM GOLDING AND HUGHES 2012)

Teachers and teaching assistants are advised to recognize the shame that underlies these behaviours. Too much attention to the behaviours will only increase feelings of shame and thus reinforce the shield. If instead teachers and teaching assistants help the child to regulate the feelings of shame with empathy and understanding the shield will weaken, and the behaviours will reduce. The child is now on a path towards the development of guilt, and the ability to respond to consequences and to make amends. Again connection has to precede correction; only in this way will the child be able to take responsibility for behaviour instead of becoming overwhelmed by this behaviour.

Summary: challenges in supporting the emotional needs of children with attachment difficulties

Managing need for dependency versus independence

- Don't be tempted to push the child to be more independent.
- The route to independence is via dependency.
- Understand the emotional age of the child and support at this age.
- Apparent 'pseudomaturity' can mask dependency needs of some children.
- Support the child to accept dependency.
- This can be challenging when it appears counter to the objective of the setting to help children be more independent.

Maintaining high boundaries and high warmth

- All children do best in an atmosphere of authoritative parenting.
- This provides warmth, support for autonomy and appropriate boundaries.
- Boundaries provide consistency, predictability, routines and consequences.
- Warmth provides nurturing support, encouraging autonomy.
- If children are to benefit from consequences and behavioural guidance, they will need support for their emotional insecurity.
- Children with attachment difficulties often have core beliefs in their own badness.
- Without a high degree of warmth from supportive adults, they are much more likely to enter a state of shame.
- Experience of shame tends to cut children off from relationships.

Managing behaviour while supporting emotional development

- The challenging behaviour of the child with complex emotional needs can oppose our expectations and values.
- Behavioural management programmes respond in a way which discourages the inappropriate behaviours and encourages alternative behaviours.
- We provide a 'correction' by rewarding a behaviour we want to increase and provide a negative consequence for a behaviour we want to reduce.
- Emotional development thrives on connection not correction.

- When we connect emotionally to a child, we recognize and understand the emotional experience which has led to the behaviour.

- Children with attachment difficulties are at particular risk of missing out on connection as their difficulties make them distrustful of emotional connection with another.

- When developing support tailored to the emotional needs of the child it is vital that connection precedes correction.

Supporting children with shame-based difficulties

- The experience of shame is part of the socialization process, via breaks in attunement leading to shame and behaviour inhibition.

- Attunement, breaks and relationship repair are healthy for children.

- When discipline is harsh, punitive or inconsistent and when relationships are not repaired, children will experience unregulated shame.

- If the healthy development of guilt does not develop, an emotion which drives us to make amends, the child gets stuck in shame.

- These children learn to put up a 'shield against the shame'; leading to defensive behaviours such as lying, minimizing, blaming others and raging.

- Too much attention to the behaviours will only increase feelings of shame and thus reinforce the shield.

- By helping the child to regulate the feelings of shame with empathy and understanding, the shield will weaken, and the behaviours will reduce.

12 Supporting Children with Multiple Difficulties

Many of the children who especially concern us in schools have complex emotional needs stemming not only from attachment difficulties but also from neurodevelopmental difficulties. These difficulties originate in a combination of early experience and genetic vulnerability. Difficult early experience can impact on neurodevelopment: the brain develops within a social environment and therefore is vulnerable to poor development when the social environment is poor.

Additionally difficult early experience can exacerbate genetic difficulties that the child was born with. All of this can be difficult to unpick and teachers and teaching assistants are often left struggling to know whether they are supporting a child with attachment difficulties, developmental difficulties or both. An educational psychologist can be helpful in advising on further assessment and providing advice about support for these children.

Fortunately many of the ideas for supporting children with attachment difficulties are also helpful for children with neurodevelopmental difficulties. Likewise ways of supporting children with neurodevelopmental problems can be helpful for children with attachment difficulties.

Children with generalized learning difficulty

The experience of a generalized learning difficulty can increase the difficulty that children have in building and maintaining relationships. Thus the risk of attachment difficulties is increased and the subsequent difficulties in attachment and relationships can cause emotional distress, leading to the development of challenging behaviours. In addition, the difficulties that the children have may make them less responsive, or less clear, in what they signal. This can affect the communication between adult and child. Learning difficulties may slow down the process of learning about relationships, and in adjusting to change and new routines.

These children may therefore have more difficulty in adjusting to and feeling secure in school. They may take longer to respond to the consistent and nurturing care that the school is providing, and they may find it difficult to communicate their distress because of both the attachment difficulty and the learning difficulty.

With these children it is important to focus on reducing emotional distress, increasing security and building relationships. As the emotional distress is reduced and relationship development is facilitated, the behavioural difficulties will also reduce (e.g. see O'Driscoll 2009).

Children with autism

Peter Hobson (2002) has identified how problems within the child or within the environment can lead to 'autistic' difficulties. Children need the mental equipment (nature) and experience of other people (nurture) to allow them to experience interpersonal relations with others.

Many children with autism do develop secure attachments in early life. For example, in one research study 50 per cent of children with autism were shown to have developed a secure attachment to their mother (Koren-Karie *et al.* 2009). However, it can be more difficult for carers to interpret signals from the children because of their social difficulties. Thus risk of attachment difficulty is increased. It might be that children with autism are more vulnerable in families where parenting difficulties are already high.

Children with attachment difficulties are similar to children with autism in responding well to a highly structured environment, with predictability and lots of preparation for change. Therefore, the use of visual calendars and social stories™ can be helpful whether the emotional difficulties the child is presenting are due to neurodevelopmental or attachment difficulties, or a combination of both.

Children with sensory integration difficulties

Young children depend on adults to provide for their sensory needs and thus to foster the development of the nervous system. Children with attachment difficulties may have missed out on important experiences, usually occurring during nurturing care, which help the sensory systems to develop and to work in an integrated way. Similarly exposure to trauma during pregnancy or early infancy can alter the way the infant's brain develops and how he or she organizes sensory experiences. Eadaoin Bhreathnach (2006) highlighted that children who have a history of separation, loss, abuse and neglect are more likely to present with both attachment and sensory processing difficulties.

This is therefore another difficulty that emerges out of a combination of genetic and environmental factors. Sensory integration is the ability of the central nervous system to organize and process input from different sensory channels to make an adaptive response (Ayres 1972). Children with difficulties in this area are not able to use sensory information easily to plan and carry out actions. This makes everyday experiences unpleasant or overwhelming. For example, a child may struggle to sit comfortably surrounded by other children, or may not be able to sit still on a chair. These difficulties can have a significant impact on a child's emotional regulation and learning.

Some children may have difficulty modulating their responses to sensory input, which means they may over- or under-respond to certain sensory experiences. These children may present with either hypersensitivity or hyposensitivity to a greater or lesser degree.

Hypersensitivity

The hypersensitive child has a low threshold for sensory input and is therefore quickly overwhelmed, leading to a strong emotional response and defensive reactions. These children may struggle with auditory or visual stimulation. Such children may, for example, respond aggressively when touched unexpectedly; they may dislike certain textures or fabrics or certain smells, or they may avoid messy tasks or areas which are visually stimulating. Similarly they may become overwhelmed quickly in noisy environments or in response to unexpected noise, and may make noise themselves to drown out these noises.

If the vestibular system is hypersensitive, children will struggle with balance and heights. They may avoid physical education and similar activities.

Hyposensitivity

The hyposensitive child has a high threshold for sensory input and therefore ignores or is relatively unaffected by sensory stimuli to which most people would respond. These children often seek out intense sensory experiences, and are therefore described as sensory seeking. Such children may, for example, be unaware that they have been touched, be constantly touching or smelling things, seek out rough and tumble play excessively. They may sit close to the television or prefer bright flashing toys. They may seek out loud noise, preferring noisy activities, and they may talk loudly themselves.

Children who have low sensitivity to proprioception may appear uncoordinated with low muscle tone. They seek out activities that involve heavy resistance, pushing and pulling or climbing, for example.

If the vestibular system is hyposensitive, the children may have exaggerated movements and seek out activities such as spinning and climbing.

Alongside the checklist observations, notice the types of movement the child is engaging in. Advice about how to help these children can be found in a range of books by Carol Stock Kranowitz and colleagues (e.g. Koomar *et al.* 2001; Kranowitz 2005). Advice can also be sought from the local paediatric occupational therapy service.

Children who demonstrate extreme non-compliance and explosive behaviour

There are a group of children who are fragile neurodevelopmentally because they have difficulties not only with compliance to adult demands but also with regulation of their behaviour. These are also examples of difficulties that can arise within the development of attachment difficulties, although at its extreme it is likely to be the result of both genetic and environmental factors. Ross Greene (2010) in his book *The Explosive Child* describes these children as being developmentally delayed in the skills of flexibility and in being able to tolerate frustration.

The root of this difficulty is poor executive functioning. Executive functioning skills are governed by frontal and prefrontal areas of the brain. Brain development in this area can be particularly influenced by lack of good early parenting experience, although some children are born genetically more at risk of these difficulties.

Difficulties in executive functioning can lead to emotional distress and frustration which is displayed through non-compliant and/or explosive behaviour. These children can have difficulties in the following areas:

- *Cognitive shifting:* this means they find it difficult to mentally adjust to changing circumstances. Imagine a child who is told to go to the reading corner ready to read with a mentor. The mentor doesn't arrive and the child then has to deal with a quick change of plan. The child is ready for reading and cannot quickly adjust to not reading after all.

- *Organization and planning:* children have increasingly sophisticated abilities to form a plan of action and to use this plan to solve a problem based on the ability to organize and plan. A child with this difficulty might find it hard to work out what to do when a problem presents itself. For example, a girl who is asked to take a message to the office, but when she arrives the office is empty, may not have the ability to work out what to do in this situation.

- *Self-regulation:* children need to be able to regulate their emotional reaction to an event well enough to be able to plan and behave in a way that reaches a goal. When you can emotionally manage a problem, you will be able to think and thus solve the problem. A boy wants to join other children in a game of football, for example. There is no obvious pause in the game so that he can join in. He needs to think about how to reach his goal of joining the game. This might be asking the children if he can join in, or waiting until a natural break occurs. If his emotional reaction to the lack of an opening, such as anxiety or frustration, is not managed, the child will not be able to think through how to reach this goal.

- *Problems with attention and impulse control:* these difficulties can make it difficult for a child to manage his or her initial impulsive reaction to a problem, in order to focus on the problem, and to attend to the important things needed to solve this problem. The child cannot filter out the unimportant so that he or she attends to what is important. A boy picks up a pencil just as a girl is reaching for it. The girl needs to inhibit her first impulse, probably to snatch the item or to push the child.

She can then focus on the problem that she has lost access to the pencil. If she cannot inhibit this impulse, she won't be able to engage in the problem solving.

These children benefit from being supported by a key adult who knows them well. This adult can spot difficulties as they arise, stepping in early to support the child, and helping him or her to develop the missing skills in the process.

Children with ADHD

Some children demonstrating the difficulties described in the previous section are diagnosed as having attention deficit hyperactivity disorder (ADHD). This is also a problem with faulty executive functioning, leading to poor attention span and impulse control, combined with excessive activity levels. As with the previous difficulties, it is hard to sort out cause from effect with these children, especially when there are known home difficulties for them. Did genetic difficulties with activity and attention contribute to poor early parenting experience or did poor early parenting experience impact on the development of these children leading to or exacerbating the activity and attention difficulties?

These children need to attend classrooms that are adapted to the difficulties that they are displaying. They need to be supported by teachers and teaching assistants who know them well, with opportunities to get outside and 'run off steam'. Research suggests that play, especially rough and tumble play, can be beneficial for these children, improving their ability to focus and concentrate (Panksepp 2007). Appropriately supervised time outside can help the child to be more successful with indoor activities.

Further advice about supporting children with attention and attachment difficulties can be found in Randy Comfort's book, *Searching to be Found* (Comfort 2008).

Children can therefore have a range of developmental difficulties alongside the difficulties more directly stemming from poor early attachment experience. The observation checklist provides structured observations of the social and emotional abilities and difficulties of the child. This information used sensitively alongside an understanding of other neurodevelopmental difficulties that the child is experiencing can help to build up a profile. This will guide staff about the special needs of the child and how to meet these. It will also prompt staff when external advice might be helpful.

Summary: working with children with multiple difficulties

Children with generalized learning difficulty

- The risk of attachment difficulties is increased and the subsequent difficulties in attachment and relationships can cause emotional distress, leading to the development of challenging behaviours.

- Children may be less responsive, or less clear, in what they signal, leading to communication difficulties between adult and child.

- Learning difficulties may slow down the process of learning about relationships, and in adjusting to change and new routines.

- They may take longer to respond to the consistent and nurturing care that the educational setting provides.

- It is important to focus on reducing emotional distress, increasing security and building relationships.

Children with autism

- Children need the mental equipment (nature) and experience of other people (nurture) to allow them to experience interpersonal relations with others.

- Many children with autism do develop secure attachments in early life.

- However, it can be more difficult for carers to interpret signals from the children because of their social difficulties, thus risk of attachment difficulty is increased.

- It might be that children with autism are more vulnerable in families where parenting difficulties are already high.

- Children with attachment difficulties are similar to children with autism in responding well to a highly structured environment, with predictability and lots of preparation for change.

- The use of visual calendars and social stories™ can be helpful, whether the emotional difficulties the child is presenting are due to neurodevelopmental or attachment difficulties, or a combination of both.

Children with sensory integration difficulties

- Children with attachment difficulties may have missed out on important experiences, usually occurring during nurturing care, which help the sensory systems to develop and to work in an integrated way.

- Exposure to trauma during pregnancy or early infancy can alter the way the infant's brain develops and how he or she organizes sensory experiences.

- Children who have a history of separation, loss, abuse and neglect are more likely to present with both attachment and sensory processing difficulties.

- Sensory integration is the ability of the central nervous system to organize and process input from different sensory channels to make an adaptive response.

- Children with difficulties in this area are not able to use sensory information easily to plan and carry out actions.

- Everyday experiences are unpleasant or overwhelming, e.g. sitting still.

- These difficulties can have a significant impact on a child's emotional regulation and learning.

- Some children may over-respond (hypersensitivity) or under-respond (hyposensitivity) to certain sensory experiences to a greater or lesser degree.

Children who demonstrate extreme non-compliance and explosive behaviour

- These are difficulties that can arise within the development of attachment difficulties, although at its extreme it is likely to be the result of both genetic and environmental factors. Brain development in this area can be particularly influenced by lack of good early parenting experience.

- These children are developmentally delayed in the skills of flexibility and in being able to tolerate frustration.

- The root of this difficulty is poor executive functioning leading to emotional distress and frustration which is displayed through non-compliant and/or explosive behaviour.

- These children can have difficulties in cognitive shifting; organization and planning; self-regulation; attention and impulse control.

- These children benefit from being supported by a key adult who knows them well.

Children with ADHD

- Faulty executive functioning leads to poor attention span and impulse control, combined with excessive activity levels.

- It is hard to sort out cause from effect with these children, especially when there are known home difficulties for the child.

- Genetic difficulties with activity and attention may contribute to poor early parenting experience.

- Poor early parenting experiences impact on the development of these children leading to or exacerbating the activity and attention difficulties.

- Education environments need to adapt to the difficulties that they are displaying.

- These children benifit form being supported by workers who know them well, with opportunities to get outside and 'run off steam'.

- Rough and tumble play can be beneficial for these children, improving their ability to focus and concentrate.

- Appropriately supervised time outside can help the child to be more successful with indoor activities.

Appendices

Appendix 1

Observation Checklist

Name of child				Date of birth	
Name of school				Start date	
				Hours attending	
Stage of SEN Code of Practice	Not applicable	School Action		School Action Plus	Statement
Other settings child attends					
Name of parents/carers				Language spoken at home	
Address					

Details of observations

The child will be observed over a few days (observation period) by a person who knows him or her well (e.g. teacher or teaching assistant). This key person might make some observations for this tool or might rely on observations that are being routinely made anyway. Further observation periods can be used to monitor progress after implementing an action plan. Different colours for different observation periods will allow ease of monitoring.

Dates of first observation period	Colour used	Key person	Factors affecting the observation (e.g. child's health, changes in the school, changes at home etc.)
Dates of second observation period (if needed)	Colour used	Key person	Factors affecting the observation (e.g. child's health, changes in the school, changes at home etc.)
Dates of third observation period (if needed)	Colour used	Key person	Factors affecting the observation (e.g. child's health, changes in the school, changes at home etc.)

1. Behaviour

		Almost always	Sometimes	As child of same age or stage of development	Sometimes	Almost always	
What is child's behaviour like?	Resists boundaries, non-compliant						Overly compliant, accepts boundaries with little fuss
	Difficult behaviour that is overly challenging						Passive but difficult behaviour that is expressed subtly
	Unpredictable, easily triggered emotional outbursts						Appears very self-contained, too good
Attention, concentration and activity levels?	Loses concentration easily						Concentration can be intense, becomes absorbed in tasks, hard to interrupt
	Impulsive, often acts without thinking						Overly controlled, rarely impulsive
	Restless, highly active						Less active than expected

Supporting evidence and comments

2. Play and task-related behaviours and relationships with peers

		Almost always	Sometimes	As child of same age or stage of development	Sometimes	Almost always	
Behaviour with other children	Possessive about playing with other children						Not interested in playing with other children
	Wants to join in but struggles to get along with others						Tends to play alone, appears isolated
	Overly controlling and bossy with other children						When does interact with another child, tends to be easily led
	Can be quite boisterous and rough towards other children. May be seen as bullying						Is often controlled or picked on by other children. Vulnerable to bullying
Play and task-related behaviour	Reluctant to engage in new play or tasks						Overly enthusiastic about new play or tasks
	Finds it difficult to settle to task						Tends to get over-involved in task to exclusion of others
	Unable to play imaginatively						Overly absorbed in imaginary world
	Overly competitive, always wants to be first						Overly timid, reluctant to join in
Supporting evidence and comments							

3. Attachment behaviours

		Almost always	Sometimes	As child of same age or stage of development	Sometimes	Almost always	
How is the child upon separation and reunion with caregiver?	Very clingy, does not want to leave caregiver						Doesn't look back, takes little notice of caregiver
	Angry or overly distressed when caregiver returns						Actively avoids and ignores caregiver
	Cries, hard to soothe. Appears not comforted						Never cries or shows emotion
How does the child behave with familiar adults?	Unusually dependent						Unusually independent
	Stays close to adult, tries to gain attention, talks a lot						Difficult to relate to, avoids eye-contact
	Very clingy, wants to be with adult all the time						Hard to get close to, or false quality to affection given
	Overly demanding and attention-needing						Overly self-reliant, undemanding, detached
	Likes to be in control/in charge						Unusually passive; tries too hard to please

✓

		Almost always	Sometimes	As child of same age or stage of development	Sometimes	Almost always	
How does the child behave with unfamiliar adults?	Overly affectionate, gets too physically close						Overly fearful, shy, wary
	Overly demanding and attention-needing						Resists friendly overtures
	Likes to be in control/in charge						Unusually passive; tries too hard to please
	Asks personal questions even though does not mean to be rude						Shows little interest in visitor
How does the child behave when experiencing minor hurts?	Appears overly distressed						Acts as if nothing has happened
	Wants lots of comfort						Appears not to need comfort
	Needs lots of soothing and resists being comforted						Appears not to need soothing

Supporting evidence and comments

4. Emotional state

		Almost always	Sometimes	As child of same age or stage of development	Sometimes	Almost always	
Current emotional state, considering any current circumstances?	Appears overly anxious, worried or distressed						No anxieties or concerns even when there is cause
	Appears overly cheerful or happy						Appears sad, withdrawn or flat
	Appears very sensitive, easily upset						Appears indifferent, doesn't show feelings
How does the child display feelings?	It is easy to tell how the child is feeling						Tends to hide feelings away. It is difficult to tell how the child is feeling
	Displays feelings only through angry, challenging behaviour						Tends not to show how he/she is feeling in the way he/she behaves
	Tends to hurt others						Tends to hurt self

Supporting evidence and comments

5. Attitude to attendance at school

		Almost always	Sometimes	As child of same age or stage of development	Sometimes	Almost always	
Attitude to attendance at school	Overly enthusiastic about attending						Overly reluctant to attend
	Does not cope well with school, appears immature						Copes well with school, but rather too grown up
	Can become very disruptive or oppositional when directed by adults						Passive but non-compliant when directed by adults

Any other comments

What works in this environment for this child?

Action Plan to Support Observation Checklist

Name of child		DOB		Code of Practice
Dates of observation				None
Involved professionals				SA
				SA+
				STATEMENT

What works well			Areas for development	

Concern	Target	How will this be achieved?	Resources	Who? Where?

Concern	Target	How will this be achieved?	Resources	Who? Where?

Concern	Target	How will this be achieved?	Resources	Who? Where?

Review date			Action plan shared with	

✔

Appendix 2

Attachment Theory and Schools

In this appendix we expand on Chapter 3 to provide a more in-depth overview of attachment theory and discuss its relevance for those caring for children in schools. An understanding of this theory of relationship development will help teachers and teaching assistants better understand the emotional needs of the children in their care.

What is attachment theory?

Attachment theory was first proposed by John Bowlby (see Bowlby 1973, 1980, 1982, 1998) and expanded with the work of Mary Main (see Main and Solomon 1986) and Mary Ainsworth (see Ainsworth *et al.* 1978). Attachment theory is essentially a theory of how children develop, with a particular focus on the influence of early relationships. The theory describes the impact this early experience has on the way the child approaches later relationships and how this influences social, emotional and cognitive development.

Attachment theory suggests that infants are born biologically predisposed to form attachment relationships with their parents and carers. In this discussion we will use the term parent to describe those who are currently parenting the children. These parent–child relationships are used by the children not only to elicit security and comfort, but also as a secure base from which to explore and learn in the world. Innate drives to attach and to explore are both present within the child. When children feel safe and secure, they will explore. If, however, their feelings of safety are threatened, the desire to explore reduces and the children will seek comfort from their parents. In this way the parent becomes an attachment figure, available to the child to provide security when needed.

Attachment and exploration

Imagine Lucy and her mum visiting the classroom for the first time. When they first arrive Lucy is wary, remaining close to her mum. Her attachment needs are high in this new environment.

Gradually Lucy begins to feel confident and she starts to explore the room. She 'homes in' on the dressing up corner and moves over to watch the children putting on the costumes. Her exploration needs are high now. At this point the school bell rings. This is mildly alarming for Lucy, who wasn't expecting it. This triggers the attachment system. Lucy returns to her mum in order to feel secure again.

Like a see-saw the attachment and exploration needs rise and fall, as attachment needs rise, exploration falls and vice versa.

The young child therefore develops a set of attachment behaviours which serve to keep the parent close when the child is experiencing increased stress. These are:

- *Proximity seeking:* the child moves closer to the parent.

- *Separation protest:* the child protests at separation from the parent by crying.

- *Secure base effect:* the child derives comfort from the presence of the parent.

These behaviours are triggered by anxiety, fear or need for comfort, for example, when:

- There is actual or threatened separation from the parent at a time when the child is experiencing insecurity.

- There are alarming conditions within the environment, the presence of someone unfamiliar, for example.

- The carer is rejecting or psychologically unavailable to the child.

- The child is feeling tired and unwell.

Children need to know that their attachment figures are available, able to sensitively meet their emotional needs. This is about the parent being not only physically present but also psychologically available – ready to respond to the child when needed.

Young children are dependent upon close contact with an attachment figure. This may be their parent, substitute carer or someone involved in providing nurture, such as a child-minder. When children are upset or distressed, they need physical contact to soothe them. As they grow older, they will still need to draw security from attachment figures but they will be able to tolerate longer periods away from them. They will also be calmed by the presence of the parents, through verbal reassurance, as well as by physical contact.

From their early experience within attachment relationships, children develop a cognitive model of how relationships work (called an internal working model). This means that they have a memory of relationships, which influences how they respond in later relationships. Their later experience will influence and modify this model, but children remain strongly influenced by their early experience. The quality of the relationship with parents will influence children's social and emotional development.

The quality of these early relationships will also impact on children when they are at school. This will influence the degree to which they can trust other adults and therefore feel safe at school. It will also influence the degree to which they can focus away from their attachment needs and attend to learning.

What are the different patterns of attachment that a child might display?

Children will develop different behavioural styles of relating to attachment figures depending upon their early experience. These are called attachment patterns and they develop in response to the sensitivity of the parenting they have received. In particular, how able and willing the parent is to understand the behaviour and emotions of the child from the child's point of view. When parents can do this, they will provide an attuned relationship with the child which provides comfort at times of distress and facilitates exploration and an interest in the world when attachment needs have been met. This experience is important for the child's emotional development, enabling him or her to learn to regulate feelings and behaviour.

Parenting

Parenting lies on a continuum between sensitive and insensitive depending on how able the parent is to recognize and respond to the needs that the child signals. This will vary from day to day but if parenting is sensitive enough of the time, the child will feel secure.

Tom falls over and cries, his sensitive parent comforts him until he is ready to return to his play. Jake falls over, but gets up unconcerned; his sensitive parent gives him a quick check over and then lets him return to play. If the parents told Tom not to make a fuss and to get back to his play or tried to excessively cuddle and comfort Jake, they would be demonstrating insensitivity.

This can be broken down further according to whether the parent is one of the following:

- *Accepting–rejecting*: how able the parent is to accept that the child has his or her own needs. The accepting parent can recognize the signals that the child is giving and accept that this is how he or she is feeling. Tom's parent accepts he needs comfort while Jake's parent accepts his need to get on with playing.

- *Cooperating–interfering*: how able the parent is to respond to the child's signals, helping the child to feel comforted or to explore in line with the needs being expressed. Tom's parent provides comfort while Jake's parent facilitates play.

- *Accessible–ignoring*: how able the parent is to remain alert and available to the child, noticing the signals that the child gives out. An accessible parent is able to engage with the child when the child needs it rather than when the parent wants to. Both Tom and Jake's parents are accessible, meeting the needs as signalled by the boys.

(see Ainsworth *et al.* 1978)

Patterns of attachment

Psychologically children develop a strategy to help them experience closeness and psychological engagement with their parents. This allows them to feel safe and to expect protection when in danger. This pattern will be adaptive for the child in relation to the parent's behaviour and degree of sensitivity. This will then reflect the quality of the attachment relationship and the way the internal working model develops. These patterns of relating therefore influence the way children respond to later relationships, including those relationships they form as they enter nursery and later at school. Children will have experienced a number of relationships before they enter school. This means that they may have a range of styles of relating, showing combinations of the patterns described below.

Perhaps confusingly there are contrasting models of the development of the attachment patterns. In this book we describe the patterns using the more traditional A B C + D model (see Figure A2.1), rather than the alternative Dynamic Maturational Model (DMM) developed by Crittenden (Crittenden *et al.* 2001; Crittenden 2008). This latter model does not recognize a disorganized pattern, preferring a focus on organization and adaptation to conditions of fear and danger. However, in both models the development of controlling behaviours to deal with perceived threat is emphasized, and it is these controlling behaviours which will be most apparent within school. (A useful discussion of these differing models can be found in Howe 2011.)

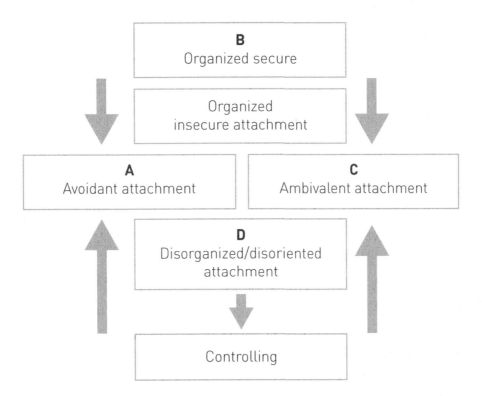

FIGURE A2.1 SUMMARY OF PATTERNS OF ATTACHMENT

Secure attachment pattern (B)

A secure attachment develops out of an attuned relationship. The parent is sensitive to the child's signals, accessible when needed, accepting and supportive of the child. Secure relationships allow children to develop trust in others and appropriate self-reliance in themselves. Securely attached children have positive expectations of themselves and others and approach the world with confidence. When these children are faced with potentially alarming situations, they will tackle them effectively or will seek help to do this.

Sophie displays a secure attachment pattern

Sophie is a quiet but confident six-year-old who enjoys playing with her friends. She likes Mum to be around, but is able to amuse herself. She likes drawing and playing with her dolls. She was a bit alarmed when a wasp flew into the room, however, and ran to Mum for help. Mum made sure the wasp was gone. Sophie, feeling safe, readily returned to her playing.

When Mum brings Sophie to school, she is keen to meet up with her friends. Mum leaves her in the playground and she walks in to school with Louise, her best friend. Sophie appears happy at school. She is happy to share and works well in a group. She relates well to the staff. She happily follows the routines that are in place and is achieving academically. If she is frustrated, she will appear cross but readily lets a member of staff help her. Generally Sophie is a cooperative, easy-going child in school.

When Sophie reaches ten years, she is increasingly independent of the need for her mum to be available in the playground before school; she continues to work both independently and as an active participant within group work. She is usually very responsive to teacher instruction.

Secure attachment in school

Children with a secure attachment pattern appear confident. Whether quiet or lively, these children will appear to relish the challenges that the school provides. They are confident to have a go, but will also seek help from the adults when needed.

Socially these children can draw on the full range of cognitive and emotional information to make sense of the social world. They are able to make friends and mix well with their peers.

The children have a good understanding of their own and others' feelings. They are developing a sense of self-efficacy, self-confidence and social competence. They can trust others and will approach others for help. They can resolve conflicts and demonstrate self-reliance. They cope with stress and frustration.

The children achieve success in school. They cope and enjoy learning tasks, suitable for their age and ability. They enjoy achieving and can cope with not knowing. They are able to use the teacher for support as needed. These children enjoy engaging with learning tasks, both on their own and supported by the adults. The children relate well to adults and engage fully with activities.

Secure attachment can be promoted by working in partnership with parents: see Figure A2.2.

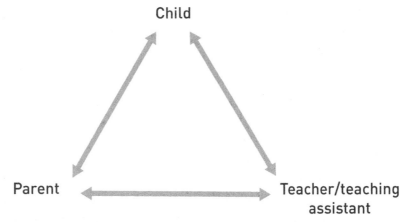

FIGURE A2.2 PARTNERSHIP WORKING TO SUPPORT A CHILD

Insecure attachment patterns

Research has demonstrated that around 60 per cent of children have a secure attachment, while 40 per cent of children develop insecure attachments (Van IJzendoorn and Sagi 1999). It should be noted therefore that insecure attachment does not necessarily mean that problems will follow. Rather, insecure attachment is a risk factor for later emotional and developmental difficulties, while secure attachment is a protective factor. However, when children have experienced early adverse environments including abuse or neglect, it is likely that they will develop more extreme insecure attachments and therefore will be at greater risk of emotional and developmental difficulties.

Insecure avoidant pattern (A)

An insecure avoidant attachment develops out of a relationship with a parent who is distant and rejecting. The parent finds it difficult to cope with the child's emotional needs and therefore is not sensitive to these needs. Overt expression of emotional distress from the child tends to lead the parent to withdraw further. As a consequence the child becomes anxious when experiencing strong feelings. The child learns to minimize attachment behaviour to maintain closeness to the parent. This is expressed through undemanding behaviour with limited displays of emotional distress. Additionally, when these children experience parents as hostile, they will demonstrate compulsively compliant behaviour being anxious to please and to do things right. When these children do feel angry, they often express this through short-lived loss of control with anger suddenly erupting. Alternatively they might show this anger through passive-aggressive behaviour. This is indirect behaviour; the child displays anger through an action that is carried out behind the adult's back.

Mark displays an avoidant attachment pattern

Mark is an independent six-year-old who makes few demands of his father. Mark will play alone, giving Dad a bright smile when he comes in. He is also keen to help his dad, frequently checking he is OK and helping him with little jobs. When Mark sees a wasp fly into the room, he keeps a wary eye on it but continues playing.

When Dad brings Mark to school, he enters confidently on his own, barely looking back as Dad leaves. He follows the rules and routines, making few demands on staff. He approaches other children but tends to hang back, waiting to be invited to join in. He enjoys running around at the fringes of their games in the outdoor area. Sometimes he falls over, but generally just picks himself up and continues with the game. Mark prefers to work on his own. He lacks confidence but does not liked to be helped. If working in a group he is quiet, tending to follow the lead of the other children. Staff rarely see Mark upset, but occasionally when he is very frustrated with something he will 'explode' with anger. He resists staff attempts to help him and is quickly back to normal.

When Mark reaches ten years, he remains seemingly independent within the classroom, his work output is usually the minimum required. Mark will just sit rather than ask for help from school staff. He continues to experience seemingly 'untriggered' outbursts from time to time.

Insecure avoidant patterns in school

These children can appear withdrawn and quiet. They rely on knowledge and ignore feelings to guide behaviours. They will generally appear more self-reliant and independent than expected for their age, and will be reluctant to turn to adults when they need help. Distress is denied or not communicated. They may try to take care of the teacher. These children can appear happy or settled much of the time. If stress builds up, the child may show a sudden and apparently inexplicable tantrum which is quickly over.

Apparently friendly careful observation can reveal that these children are relatively isolated as they lack emotional engagement with other children or with adults. They avoid intimacy.

The children may appear more focused on activities than on people. They can focus on learning to avoid relationships. While achievement can lead to some sense of accomplishment, they fear failure. They can therefore focus more on what they can't do than what they can do. They resist help from the teacher but also lack confidence in their own ability. The child finds it easier to engage with activities than to relate to adults. These children are less able to use the teacher or teaching assistant to support and help them with the task.

Insecure ambivalent pattern (C)

An insecure ambivalent attachment develops out of a relationship with a parent who is inconsistent and unpredictable. These insensitive parents will sometimes meet their children's needs but this is more dependent on their mood than the children's need. The child learns to maximize attachment behaviour to elicit care. This is expressed through coercive, demanding and clingy behaviour. Emotional distress can be extreme and there is a resistance to being soothed and comforted.

Kelly displays an ambivalent attachment pattern

Kelly is a needy six-year-old who has not yet learnt to play alone. She follows her parents around the house, rarely settling to anything. If a visitor arrives, Kelly tries to insert herself between her parents and the visitor. Sometimes Mum, exasperated by this behaviour, will insist that Kelly play by herself for a time. When Kelly sees the wasp fly into the room, she screams and shouts. When Mum arrives Kelly clings to her. She will not settle even when Mum shows her that the wasp has now gone.

Kelly is not confident when brought to school. She tends to cling to her parents and does not want to be left. Once they have gone Kelly 'attaches' herself to a member of staff. She is demanding and 'attention-needing'. She talks constantly, often asking questions repetitively but not paying any attention to the answers. She likes to stay close to the staff member, not wanting her to go out of sight. She is possessive and jealous when other children want to talk to this member of staff.

Kelly will not work independently, always seeking assistance even when she does not need it. If working in a group Kelly quickly falls out with the other children as she tries to stay the centre of attention. If she falls or bumps herself, Kelly is inconsolable, clinging to the staff member who comes to help her.

By the time that Kelly has reached ten years, she has developed skills in drawing funny pictures and making jokes and uses this to make her peers laugh and get adult attention – whatever the cost. At breaktimes she finds excuses to stay in the school and 'help' staff rather than mix with her peers.

Insecure ambivalent pattern in school

These children tend to make their presence known. They are preoccupied with relationships, alert to the availability of others. They therefore have an obsessive need for adult attention. They will therefore appear attention-needing, and find it difficult to settle by themselves or with groups of children. They will sometimes talk excessively, or act as a 'class clown' in order to maintain the focus of adult attention.

Concentrating and focusing on tasks is difficult as they remain hypervigilant to what the adults are doing. These children are very focused on feelings and therefore find it difficult to attend to the rules and structure of the classroom. They therefore find it difficult to follow rules and to learn from consequences. They have poor understanding of cause and effect.

The children rely on feelings rather than knowledge to guide their behaviour. They need attention and approval to feel secure. This leads to enmeshed and entangled relationships. They constantly keep others involved in the relationship through coercive behaviours. They can escalate confrontation in order to hold the attention of others. They view the teacher as either all good or all bad, and may oscillate between these depending on their immediate feeling.

The children do not expect friendships to go well as they lack social competence. They find it hard to maintain friendships and can be clingy and possessive. They are oversensitive to signs of rejection.

Learning is difficult as they have poor concentration to tasks and are easily distracted. They are highly dependent and therefore need a lot of attention. They remain overly focused on the relationship with the teacher or teaching assistant and this can be at the expense of learning. The children find it difficult to engage with the activity because they are busy making sure the teacher or teaching assistant is noticing them. These children find it difficult to engage in activities without adult support.

Disorganized/disorientated and controlling attachment pattern (D)

A disorganized/disorientated and controlling attachment develops out of a relationship within which the parent is frightened of or frightening to the child. Parents can be frightened of their children when they have their own history of trauma associated with being parented. The act of parenting their child triggers memories of their own fear, and they become absorbed with this memory and thus unavailable to the child. This is as frightening to the child as more overt acts such as hitting or shouting at the child.

In these cases the parent is both the source of fear and the potential for safety. This dilemma causes extreme anxiety in the children, which is demonstrated in young children through bizarre behaviours such as freezing, approaching with the head turned away or unusual movements. While children will have organized strategies to engage with their parents, at times of extreme stress they are unable to organize their behaviour in a way that allows them to obtain emotional support.

As they grow older, disorganized children solve the dilemma of having a parent who is a source both of comfort and of fear by taking control of the relationship. They do not trust in the parent so they become controlling in their behaviour. This forces the other person into a predictable although sometimes angry pattern of responding. The child feels both powerful and frightened.

Daniel displays a disorganized-controlling attachment pattern

Daniel is an angry, hyperactive six-year-old who is exhausting to his mother. He is on the go all the time, playing loud active games. He frequently puts himself in danger and needs constant supervision. He is bossy, telling his mother what she must do. When she asks him to do something he ignores her. When Daniel sees the wasp enter the room, he runs around chasing it. When Mum tries to remove the wasp, Daniel gets angry, telling her to leave it alone.

Daniel arrives at school and everyone knows it. He comes in loudly and tries to tell the other children what to do. When staff approach, he becomes angry towards them. Difficult to contain indoors, Daniel prefers to be outside, running around and chasing the other children. He does not like to come back indoors and it is difficult to help him adjust to being back in the classroom. Daniel does not settle to his work; he is too busy seeing what everyone else is doing. He can explode with anger, and often has to be taken out of the classroom.

Occasionally he will spend time drawing – he likes to draw soldiers in battle, frequently with lost limbs and lots of blood. Soon, however, he is running around again or fighting with one of the other children. When staff try to intervene, they can be physically attacked.

When he reaches ten years, Daniel will often run out of the classroom when he feels challenged by work or relationships. He has difficulty accepting teacher authority and will respond with verbal and occasionally physical aggression.

> ## Elaine displays a disorganized and withdrawn attachment pattern
>
> Elaine is a quiet, withdrawn six-year-old who spends a lot of time in her bedroom. As her mother approaches, Elaine is vigilant, keeping an eye on her. At times she will approach her mother, as if to check that she is all right. She is very compliant, doing as she is told and urgently trying to help her mother with household jobs. When Elaine sees the wasp in the room, she runs to Mum and then quickly away again. She is clearly distressed, but appears confused about whether to go to Mum for help or not.
>
> Elaine arrives at school late. She appears unconcerned when Mum goes but remains hypervigilant, watching what is going on around her but not able to settle to her work either with or without staff. At other times Elaine appears quiet and 'switched off' as she sits at a table paying little attention to what is going on around her.
>
> This behaviour pattern continues when she reaches ten years.

Within the DMM, attachment researchers have shown how these controlling patterns of behaviour are organized around the self-reliant avoidant and coercive ambivalent patterns of relating. Children may tend towards one or the other of these or show combinations of both (see Crittenden *et al.* 2001).

> ## Controlling avoidant patterns
>
> The child inhibits strong negative feelings of anxiety, fear or the need for comfort. The older child may also display false positive feelings to hide negative feelings.
>
> Children with these patterns tend to be withdrawn, unusually compliant and anxiously eager to please. As they experience increased stress, they become compulsively self-reliant and sometimes even care-giving towards their parent.

> ## Controlling ambivalent patterns
>
> The child alternates between displaying anger and vulnerability. The parent is caught in a trap of coercive interactions. If the parent ignores or habituates to the child's behaviour, the child will increase their demanding and 'attention-needing' behaviour including provocative behaviour (doing the thing the parent most doesn't want them to do) and risk-taking behaviour (if I am in danger will you rescue me?). In this way the child maintains adult attention.
>
> As they experience increased stress, they become even more obsessively preoccupied with adult attention becoming more controlling in their use of aggressive and coy behaviours.

Disorganized-controlling children in school

Whether quiet and withdrawn or loud and aggressive, these children make their presence felt by the way that they maintain control within relationships. Others tend to feel quickly manipulated. They demonstrate a diminished range of emotions, lacking the contentment and joy in activities of other children and appearing anxious much of the time. They are frequently afraid but tend to mask this through more aggressive or powerful behaviours. They can be highly disruptive in school as they demonstrate highly compulsive or obsessive behaviours which allow them to hold on to a rigid control. This may be demonstrated through a compulsive need to stay self-reliant, within which the child appears compliant but resists attempts to be helped or comforted. Some children try to take on a pseudomature care-giving role within the classroom, while others demonstrate more obsessive preoccupations with being noticed through a combination of aggressive and coy behaviours. These children are hypervigilant to what is going on around them, making it difficult to concentrate or attend to a task. Many of these children remain in a hyper-aroused state, but some children cope with excessive feelings of stress by dissociating – appearing 'switched-off'.

Relationships can cause distress with little provocation, leading to violent anger and anxious dependence. Strong feelings are overwhelming, and they find it hard to understand, distinguish or control emotions in themselves or others.

While some children remain reluctant to engage with the other children, many of these children seek friendships, but their immaturity and rigid controlling style of relating to other children can lead to social isolation.

In the classroom these children tend to be anxious and inattentive. They have poor stress tolerance, which detracts from learning. Their need to maintain feelings of being in control overrides learning as they provoke, bully or challenge others. The child feels very anxious, preventing engagement in activities. Often the anxiety is masked by angry or aggressive behaviours as the child tries to control the teacher or teaching assistant. These children find relating to adults and engagement with activities difficult.

Patterns of non-attachment

A small proportion of children have been severely neglected or raised in an institution with multiple caregivers. These children have had no experience of an early attachment relationship. Without this experience they will not be able to develop a selective attachment. Having no early attachment experience, they do not know how to draw support from the people caring for them. These children can be disinhibited. They are indiscriminate in who they go to, being friendly to anyone but unable to engage in a mutually satisfying relationship with their parent. Alternatively they can be inhibited, being fearful of others and not approaching anyone when distressed.

Katie displays signs of non-attachment

Katie is a quiet, but apparently contented child. She potters around, flitting from activity to activity. When her carer is in the room she tends to ignore her. When visitors arrive, she goes over to them and chats to them as if she has always known them. If distressed Katie fusses, but is difficult to soothe, often pushing the carer away as she attempts to respond, while simultaneously crying out to her. Katie pays no attention to the wasp in the room; she remains absorbed in pouring water from cup to cup in her tea set.

At school Katie appears contented but quite oblivious of what is going on around her. She wanders from activity to activity taking little notice of the other children. When a visitor comes into the classroom, Katie goes over to her and takes her by the hand. The visitor crouches down and talks to her, Katie turns away and wanders up to one of the other adults, again taking hold of their hand. As the other children gather their things together in preparation for going home, Katie is still wandering around picking up materials that the adults are trying to put away. As she gets older, Katie continues to appear 'unaware' of her surroundings, both in terms of her peers and tasks set. She has great difficulty in settling to and completing activities and appears surprised when adults are frustrated with her limited work output.

Non-attachment within school

These children are relatively few compared to other children with attachment difficulties. For a child to have non-attachment, an experience of severe neglect, institutional care or a large number of placement moves will be apparent in the early history. These children are notable in school by a lack of connection with adults, appearing even 'autistic' at times. This has been termed a quasi-autism to emphasize the acquired nature of the difficulties because of the early difficulties (Rutter *et al.* 2009). The children may be very withdrawn, although more usually they appear highly sociable, approaching anyone for comfort, but appearing dissatisfied by the contact with an adult. These children generally appear very immature, and respond more like younger children, tending to get on with their own thing, appearing unaware of normal rules and routines.

Summary: insecure attachment patterns

Insecure avoidant pattern

Carer ⟷ Child

- Distant and rejecting.
- Finds it difficult to cope with the child's emotional needs.

Child ⟷ Adult

- Withdrawn or quiet.
- More self-reliant than peers of same age.
- Less likely to turn to parent or teacher for support and help.
- Can appear isolated, or friendships lack depth.
- Apparent indifference to uncertainty in new situations.
- Finds physical closeness threatening.
- Inexplicable tantrums or outbursts – appear from nowhere, which can be quickly be over.
- More likely to be focused on 'doing' than relationships with people.

Insecure ambivalent pattern

Carer ⟷ Child

- Carer will sometimes meet the child's needs depending on their own mood. Therefore, unpredictably available.

Child ⟷ Adult

- High level of anxiety and uncertainty.
- Attention-needing.
- Hypervigilant to what adults are doing.
- May talk excessively, or act as a 'clown' in order to keep adult's attention.
- Accept negative or positive attention from adults.
- Difficulties attempting the task if unsupported.

- Difficulty concentrating and focusing.

- Poor understanding of cause and effect.

- May present as highly articulate but this does not correlate with achievement levels.

Disorganized/disorientated and controlling attachment pattern

Carer ⟷ Child

- Parent is frightened of or frightening to the child.

- May be because they were frightened as a child so become unresponsive when their child needs them the most.

- May be overtly frightening to the child by exposing them to family violence, odd behaviour or harsh discipline. May be abusive or neglectful.

Child ⟷ Adult

- Sees the parent as both the potential source of comfort and terror – 'I need you, but you frighten me.'

- May react to unseen triggers.

- Very controlling in their relationships.

- May be hyper-aroused or dissociated for much of the time.

- Their early brain development has developed over-responsive fight-or-flight reactions, leaving a diminished capacity to concentrate or think.

- May be unable to accept being taught, and/or unable to 'permit' others to know more than they do as this triggers overwhelming feelings of humiliation.

- Struggle in relatively unsupervised settings such as the playground or moving between lessons.

Appendix 3
Glossary

ADHD

Attention deficit hyperactivity disorder (ADHD) is the diagnosis given to a range of difficulties that children can display because they have difficulty attending to and staying focused on a task, controlling impulses and regulating their activity levels.

Affect matching

Affect is the outward expression of the emotion being experienced. These affects are conveyed through non-verbal patterns marked by the intensity of expression, the quality of the voice and gestures or movements being made. Affect matching involves one person matching these non-verbal expressions in the other. This is how empathy and understanding of the other's inner experience is conveyed. One person experiences the emotion, expressing this through affect; the other person expresses his or her understanding and empathy for this experience by matching this affect.

Ambivalent attachment

The young child develops ambivalent-resistant attachment when a parent is experienced as inconsistent and unpredictable. The child learns to maximize displays of emotion in order to maintain the parent's availability and thus appears very attention-needing. This early experience of an inconsistent parent leads to an expectation that other adults, such as teachers and nursery workers, will also be inconsistent, leading to the attention-needing behaviours also appearing in the classroom.

Attachment

Attachment is an affectional bond that develops from a child to the parent or attachment figure. This leads to an attachment pattern, a style of relating to carers and other significant adults based on the early experience of attachment relationships.

Attachment difficulties

When a child experiences difficulties in experiencing security and comfort from a caregiver, the child develops an insecure attachment. This increases the risk that the child will experience difficulties in feeling secure with alternative caregivers and other significant adults. Children experiencing caregivers as frightening are at most risk of attachment difficulties.

Attuned relationship

An attuned relationship is an emotional connection between two people in which one person mirrors or matches the vitality and affect (externally displayed mood) of the other. When an adult gets in to an attuned relationship with the child, the adult will be able to co-regulate the emotional experience of the child, soothing high arousal and stimulating low arousal.

Autism

Autism is a diagnosis given to children who display a pattern of difficulties in social communication, language and imaginative play. Onset is before three years of age. It is recognized that children can display autistic difficulties in different ways and therefore an autism spectrum is described.

Avoidant attachment

The child develops avoidant attachment when a parent is experienced as rejecting. The child learns to minimize displays of emotion in order to maintain parent availability, and thus appears self-reliant. This early experience of a rejecting parent leads to an expectation that other adults, such as teachers and nursery workers, will also be rejecting, leading to the self-reliant behaviours also appearing in the classroom.

Behavioural management

Behavioural management is a set of strategies based on social learning principles that are designed to influence the behaviour of the child. The child is rewarded for good behaviour and given consequences for bad behaviour in order to increase good and reduce bad behaviours. An over-reliance on behavioural management can lead to too much focus on behaviour and not enough on relationship. The child feels influenced, or coerced, by the other with little opportunity to influence back.

Chronological age

The chronological age of a person reflects the passage of time. For example, if a child has lived for six years, his or her chronological age is also six years.

Coercive behaviour

Coercive behaviour is displayed in order to ensure a particular reaction from others. The behaviour compels others to behave in a particular way.

Cognitive

Cognitive or conscious thinking processes take place in the cortex of the brain, and are central to learning.

Compliant behaviour

Compliant behaviour is performed in order to please another person, that is, to fit in with another person's wishes.

Compulsive behaviour

Compulsive behaviour is governed by an impulse to do something in order to maintain feelings of safety. Children who have to wash their hands whenever they touch a door handle would be demonstrating compulsive behaviour.

Appendix 3: Glossary   141

Controlling behaviour

Controlling behaviour is performed in order to feel in control within a relationship, because the behaviour causes a predictable response in the other person. Controlling behaviours interfere with the development of reciprocal relationships because the child seeks to influence others without being influenced by them.

Developmental delay

Developmental delay is when a child's abilities are immature for the child's chronological age. Children can be developmentally delayed globally, across all areas of development (generalized learning difficulty), or specifically in some areas of development but not others (specific learning difficulty).

Disinhibited

Indiscriminately friendly but superficial behaviours usually relate to an inability to engage in mutually satisfying relationships. A child is disinhibited when he or she approaches strangers and seeks a cuddle or sits on their lap. Similarly a child who discloses personal information to a visitor to the classroom would be described as disinhibited.

Disorganized-controlling attachment

The child develops disorganized-controlling attachment when a parent is experienced as frightening or frightened. The child experiences difficulty organizing his or her behaviour at times of stress. As they grow older, these children learn to control relationships to force predictability. This early experience of a frightening parent leads to an expectation that other adults, such as teachers, will also be frightening. This leads to the controlling behaviours also appearing in the classroom.

Dissociation

Dissociation is a term to describe the process by which a person defends against overwhelming stress by cutting off from conscious awareness what is being sensed or felt. At its extreme the person cuts off from contact with others or the world, becoming numb, unfeeling or unaware. Dissociation reduces the ability to make sense of self or others.

Emotional age

Emotional age is the age level at which the child's emotional needs are expressed. This can be discrepant from the chronological age, represented as emotional immaturity or emotional maturity.

Emotional co-regulation

The capacity to regulate emotion is influenced by the experience of co-regulation. This occurs when adults interact with children to help them to manage their emotion and emotional arousal.

Emotional dysregulation

Dysregulation represents a lack of regulatory capacity. It occurs when individuals fail to control and modulate emotions and emotional arousal. The emotion overwhelms them, controlling them rather than them being in control of the emotion. A child who feels angry and physically attacks another child in this rage is demonstrating emotional dysregulation.

Emotional regulation

Emotional regulation is the capacity to control and modulate emotions and emotional arousal. A child who feels angry but is able to soothe him or herself and take appropriate action is demonstrating good emotional regulation.

Empathy

Empathy is an ability to imagine and share what another is experiencing. By identifying what another is thinking or feeling, we can respond to that person with an appropriate emotion of our own. A child recognizing that another child is hurt may feel upset for the child and therefore seek to comfort him or her. Empathy is at the heart of relationship, as without empathy we cannot influence and be influenced by another.

Executive functioning

Psychologists use the term executive functioning to define a group of brain processes which are responsible for a range of cognitive processes including attention, planning, flexibility and impulse inhibition.

Generalized learning difficulty

See developmental delay.

Hyper-arousal

Hyper-arousal describes arousal which is extreme for the situation. A person is hyper-aroused when he or she responds to stress with a high state of arousal. This is an automatic response to perceived threat or danger, marked by increase in heart rate and a fight-or-flight response.

Hypersensitivity

A person is hypersensitive when he or she has a low threshold for sensory input. The individual is easily overwhelmed by sensory input and reacts defensively to it with strong negative emotion.

Hypervigilant

A person is hypervigilant when he or she constantly scans the environment for threats. When such individuals are in a state of hypervigilance, they will show enhanced attention to what is happening on the periphery while having difficulties focusing on what is happening in front of them.

Hypo-arousal

Hypo-arousal describes arousal which is less than would be expected for a situation. A person is hypo-aroused when he or she responds to stress with a low state of arousal. It is therefore an under-responsiveness with minimal reactions to stimuli.

Hyposensitivity

A person is hyposensitive when he or she has a high threshold for sensory input. The individual ignores or is relatively unaffected by sensory stimuli which most people would respond to. This individual may seek intense sensory stimulation.

Impulsive behaviour

Impulsive behaviour occurs without thinking. An impulsive individual does not 'look before leaping'. Impulse control requires that a person thinks about the consequences that might occur following the behaviour, and inhibits the action if the consequence is unacceptable.

Inhibited behaviour

An inhibited individual shows restraint in his or her behaviour. A shy individual can be described as socially inhibited.

Innate drive

An innate drive describes an instinct leading to behaviour that does not need to be learnt. The drive to attach is an innate drive, a child needs no learning to attach to parents, and the child will attach even if the parent is abusive or frightening in some way. The instinct is not easily overridden.

Interactive repair

Interactive repair is a psychological term used to describe the behaviour when one individual wants to become close to another following an episode when closeness between them was lost. It is important for healthy child development that adults re-establish a positive emotional connection between themselves and a child (attunement) following a time when the relationship was ruptured, either because of the behaviour of the child or of the parent. This is also called relationship repair.

Internal working model (IWM)

IWM is a term used in attachment theory to describe cognitive models or templates of the attachment relationships that a child has experienced. This model influences how the child will respond to future relationships.

Neurodevelopmental difficulty

Neurodevelopmental difficulty arises when neural development has been impaired in some way. The brain and nervous system have not developed optimally leading to difficulties in functioning.

Non-compliant behaviour

A person is non-compliant when he or she behaves in a way that is counter to the wishes of another person. The individual behaves in a particular way in order to thwart another person. A child who continues to walk around the classroom when asked to sit down is demonstrating non-compliant behaviour.

Obsessive behaviour

Obsessive behaviour is governed by a preoccupation with certain ideas or needs. A child is demonstrating obsessional behaviour when he or she continually approaches the teacher and asks if Mummy is going to collect him or her today, despite already being reassured of this fact.

Passive-aggressive

Passive-aggressive describes the expression of anger towards others through indirect acts of aggression, which happen behind the other's back. For example, a child might experience anger towards another child but does not express this anger directly. Instead when no one is looking, he or she steals the child's lunch box and damages it.

Pattern of attachment

The stable pattern of relating to an attachment figure and other significant adults develops in response to the way that the attachment needs of the child have been met by the caregiver early in life.

Protective behaviours

Protective behaviours is a practical approach to help people to experience personal safety, which is easily adapted to use in schools. It is an approach that can be used with individual children or as part of a class-based activity. It helps children to understand when they are not feeling safe and to seek help from a network of support at these times.

Proximity seeking

Proximity seeking is a term used in attachment theory to describe behaviour that is displayed in order to achieve closeness to an attachment figure. This increases feelings of safety and security for the child.

Pseudomaturity

Pseudomaturity is a term used to describe a person who behaves in a way that is more mature than he or she is emotionally ready for. A six-year-old child trying to cook a meal for his three-year-old sibling would be described as demonstrating pseudomature behaviour.

Reflectivity

Reflectivity is a cognitive ability that requires the individual to notice, think about and understand experience. A child who can talk about visiting the zoo at the weekend, explaining both what happened and how he or she felt about this is demonstrating reflectivity. For example, a girl might say that she visited the lion enclosure and that she felt scared of the lions.

Relationship-based play

Relationship-based play is modelled on healthy parent–infant relationships. The focus of the play is the relationship and enjoying being together. This allows the child to:

- feel safe, calm and comforted

- re-establish trust

- learn that it is good to be a child and safe to play

- learn the pleasure of joyful engagement

- enhance self-esteem

- feel more confident and competent

- develop skills in all areas of development.

This type of play has been recommended for children with attachment difficulties. It also forms the basis of Theraplay® (Booth and Jernberg 2010). This is a therapy designed to enhance the relationship between the child and parent.

Relationship repair

See interactive repair.

Secondary trauma

Working with someone who has been traumatized can result in secondary trauma. This is when the carer or teacher develops symptoms, as if they have been traumatized themselves.

Secure attachment

The child develops secure attachment when a parent is experienced as sensitive and responsive to his or her emotional needs. The child learns trust in others and appropriate self-reliance. This early experience of a sensitive parent leads to an expectation that other adults, such as teachers and nursery workers, will also be sensitive. The child is able to demonstrate age-appropriate self-reliance, seeking help from the adult when needed.

Secure base

Secure base is a term used in attachment theory to describe an adult being used as a source of security for the child. A secure base occurs when a child is able to feel secure with a parent or significant adult and is therefore able to engage in confident exploration.

Self-esteem

Self-esteem describes how people perceive themselves, their sense of their own worth. The opinion we hold about ourselves leads to our self-esteem. High self-esteem suggests that we perceive ourselves positively while low self-esteem represents a low opinion of ourselves and our worth to others.

Self-reliant

Self-reliant describes the ability to depend upon the self. Ideally self-reliance is balanced with the ability to use support from others when available. A young child who is able to sit and eat an apple is demonstrating appropriate self-reliance. If the child attempts to cut up the apple without seeking help, and the task is beyond him or her, this child would be described as being inappropriately self-reliant.

Sensory integration

Sensory integration describes the ability of the brain to take in information from the senses and to use this information in a joined-up way.

Sensory systems

The senses provide us with the information we need to function in the world. We have seven sensory systems:

- the tactile system (touch)
- proprioception (body sense)
- vestibular system (balance)
- auditory system (sound)
- visual system (sight)
- olfactory system (smell)
- gustation (taste).

Separation protest

Separation protest is a term used in attachment theory. It describes the behaviour that a secure child displays when accessibility to an attachment figure is threatened. A very young child might cry or crawl after the adult. An older child might call out or try to call him or her back.

Shame

Shame is a complex emotional state within which a person experiences negative feelings about him or herself – a feeling of being not good enough. Shame develops as part of the normal socialization process for young children. A child displays an unacceptable behaviour, the adult disciplines the child. The break in attunement between the child and adult is experienced as shame because the relationship has been disrupted. Shame is uncomfortable for children and therefore children will learn to limit shame-inducing behaviours. In this sense it is protective, because it helps children to behave in a way that is safe, socially acceptable and helps them to develop relationships. However, the child also needs experience of the adult repairing the relationship following the break in attunement. This communication that the child is still loved is an important part of healthy child development allowing the child to develop the capacity for emotional and behavioural regulation and learn to express appropriate and inhibit inappropriate behaviours.

Splitting

Splitting is a psychoanalytic term used to describe the process whereby when someone can't cope with ambivalent feelings about others they compartmentalize those people as all good or all bad. An example of splitting would be when a child describes his or her mother as wonderful and his or her father as hateful, without being able to see elements of good and bad in each.

Transitional object

Transitional object is a psychological term to describe the use of a toy or object by a child to 'stand in' for a parent or significant adult, while being separated from him or her. The object has a special significance which helps the child to know that he or she is still being kept in mind by the parent despite them not being together.

Unconditional positive regard

Unconditional positive regard describes acceptance and positive feelings for another without reservation or judgement. These feelings towards the other are not conditional upon any particular behaviour from the other. A parent demonstrates unconditional love to a child when he or she continues to love the child despite any challenging behaviour that the child is displaying. The parent loves the child no matter what.

Wondering aloud

A supportive adult can 'wonder aloud' to help children make sense of their experience, especially their inner emotional life. This is modelled on the way parents talk to their infants, wondering about how they are feeling linked to the behaviour being displayed. For example, a teaching assistant might wonder: 'I wonder if Michael is feeling very cross because he had to leave the computer. He was really enjoying this session and he is sad that it has ended.' In order to do this the adult has to mentalize – taking the perspective of the child in order to understand how the child is feeling underneath the behaviour which is an expression of these feelings.

Appendix 4
Glossary for UK Education System

Code of Practice

The Special Educational Needs (SEN) Code of Practice provides guidance which sets out process and procedures to meet the needs of children. This help is provided through a step-by-step or 'graduated approach':

- *Early Years or School Action:* this is a status of need assigned to a child when he or she is identified by staff as having additional needs that require intervention. The school or setting provides interventions that are additional to or different from those provided as part of the usual curriculum. An individual education plan (IEP) is written for the child.

- *Early Years or School Action Plus:* this is a status of need assigned to a child when staff require support from an outside agency. The school or setting is provided with advice or support from outside specialists, such as educational psychologists and specialist teacher advisers. This provides alternative interventions to use with the child. This additional support is reflected in a new IEP.

- *Statement of Special Educational Needs:* this is a legal document that sets out a child's special educational needs and the additional help he or she should receive. It will be based upon statutory assessment of the child's needs, and is reviewed annually. The statement will link with the individual education plan for the child.

Early Years Foundation Stage (EYFS)

EYFS is a comprehensive statutory framework that sets the standards for the learning, development and care of children from birth to five years. This framework was revised in Spring 2012.

Early years settings

The UK government funds providers to deliver early education to preschool children via a range of early years settings including schools, nurseries, day nurseries and family centres.

Educational psychologist (EP)

An educational psychologist is a chartered psychologist often trained as both a teacher and a psychologist. EPs are employed by the local authority to carry out specialist assessment with children and to give advice and support to teachers and parents on how a child's needs in school can be met.

Inclusion

Inclusion represents the educating of children with special educational needs, together with children who do not have special educational needs, in mainstream schools, wherever possible. Early years and childcare settings receive support from an area inclusion coordinator. This role is to work with settings to ensure that all children, whatever their needs, are included in a full range of activities and learning experiences.

Individual education plan (IEP)

An IEP is a tool to aid with planning, teaching and reviewing progress. The plan sets out the short-term targets that education staff will work towards for an individual child, and strategies that can be used to meet these targets.

Key person

A member of staff is given the role of forming a special relationship with a child so that he or she can help the child to feel safe in school, and can support the child emotionally, socially and educationally. The key person is often a teaching assistant (learning support assistant), designated by the school to provide support to an individual child.

Key stages

The National Curriculum in England, Wales and Northern Ireland defines five key stages. These are:

- Foundation Stage: (age 3 to end of reception year, which is pre-Year 1)

- Key Stage 1: Years 1 and 2 (up to age 7)

- Key Stage 2: Years 3, 4, 5 and 6 (age 7 to 11)

- Key Stage 3: Years 7, 8 and 9 (age 11 to 14)

- Key Stage 4: Years 10 and 11 (age 14 to 16).

Key Stages 1 and 2 are taught in primary schools and Key Stages 3 and 4 are usually taught in secondary schools. Most pupils transfer from primary to secondary school at age 11 years. However, a system of middle schools also exists in some areas: here pupils are transferred from primary school to middle school at either 8 or 9 years of age, then on to secondary education at age 12 or 13 years.

Scotland has a different, flexible qualification framework that is separate from the National Curriculum-based framework used in England, Wales and Northern Ireland. This curriculum is divided into the 5–14 Curriculum and the Standard Grade for 14- to 16-year-olds.

Preschool forum or preschool special educational needs service

The preschool preventative service identifies children who need additional support before starting school and in the transition to school.

Provision map

A provision map documents the range of supports available for pupils with special education needs, to assist with the planning process for individual pupils. Some schools use provision mapping while other school's use individual education plans. These serve the same funtion.

Social and Emotional Aspects of Learning (SEAL)

The SEAL programme was published by the Department for Education and Skills (DfES) in 2005 to provide a curriculum resource for primary schools to help children's social, emotional and behavioural development.

Special educational needs (SEN)

Children have special educational needs if they have a learning difficulty which requires special educational provision to be made for them.

Special educational needs coordinator (SENCO)

The SENCO is the education practitioner in the school who has been designated as responsible for coordinating the help given to children in the school or early years setting who have special educational needs.

Teaching assistant (TA)

Sometimes called a learning support assistant, the teaching assistant is a non-teacher employed by the school to provide support for children with special education needs or disabilities. The TA will work closely with an individual pupil or with a group of pupils to support individual needs. The TA may be employed as a key person for a child with attachment difficulties.

References

Ainsworth, M.D.S., Blehar, M.C., Waters, E. and Wall, S. (1978) *Patterns of Attachment: A Psychological Study of the Strange Situation.* Hillsdale, NJ: Erlbaum.

Ayres, J.A. (1972) *Sensory Integration and Learning Disorder.* Los Angeles, CA: Western Psychological Services.

Bhreathnach, E. (2006) The Just Right State Programme. Unpublished document.

Bombèr, L.M. (2007) *Inside I'm Hurting: Practical Strategies for Supporting Children with Attachment Difficulties in School.* London: Worth Publishing.

Bombèr, L.M. (2011) *What about Me? Inclusive Strategies to Support Pupils with Attachment Difficulties Make It through the School Day.* London: Worth.

Booth, P.B. and Jernberg, A.M. (2010) *Theraplay: Helping Parents and Children Build Better Relationships through Attachment-Based Play.* San Francisco, CA: Jossey-Bass.

Bowlby, J. (1973) *Attachment and Loss, Volume II: Separation, Anxiety and Anger.* New York: Basic Books (1975, Harmondsworth: Penguin).

Bowlby, J. (1980) *Attachment and Loss, Volume III: Loss, Sadness and Depression.* New York: Basic Books (1981, Harmondsworth: Penguin).

Bowlby, J. (1982) *Attachment and Loss, Volume I: Attachment.* London: Hogarth Press; New York: Basic Books (original work published 1969).

Bowlby, J. (1998) *A Secure Base: Clinical Applications of Attachment Theory.* London: Routledge (original work published 1988).

Cairns, K. and Stanway, C. (2004) *Learn the Child: Helping Looked After Children to Learn.* London: BAAF (British Association for Adopting and Fostering).

Comfort, R.L. (2008) *Searching to be Found: Understanding and Helping Adopted and Looked After Children with Attention Difficulties.* London: Karnac.

Crittenden, P.M. (2008) *Raising Parents: Attachment, Parenting and Child Safety.* Cullompton, UK: Willan.

Crittenden, P.M., Landini, A. and Claussen, A.H. (2001) 'A Dynamic-Maturational Approach to Treatment of Maltreated Children.' In J.N. Hughes, A.M. La Greca and J.C. Conoley (eds) *Handbook of Psychological Services for Children and Adolescents.* Oxford: Oxford University Press.

Department for Education (2012) *Early Years Foundation Stage.* Available at www.education.gov.uk/schools/teachingandlearning/curriculum/a0068102/early-years-foundation-stage-eyfs (accessed 27 July 2012).

Geddes, H. (2006) *Attachment in the Classroom: The Links Between Children's Early Experience, Emotional Well-Being and Performance in School.* London: Worth Publishing.

Gerhardt, S. (2004) *Why Love Matters: How Affection Shapes a Baby's Brain.* Hove, UK: Bruner-Routledge.

Golding, K.S. and Hughes, D.A. (2012) *Creating Loving Attachments: Parenting with PACE to Nurture Confidence and Security in the Troubled Child.* London: Jessica Kingsley Publishers.

Greene, R.W. (2010) *The Explosive Child: A New Approach for Understanding and Parenting Easily Frustrated, Chronically Inflexible Children,* 2nd edn. New York: HarperPaperbacks.

Hetherington, E.M. and Parke, R.D. (1993) *Child Psychology: A Contemporary Viewpoint,* 3rd edn. New York: McGraw-Hill.

Hobson, P. (2002) *The Cradle of Thought: Exploring the Origins of Thinking.* London: Macmillan.

Howe, D. (2011) *Attachment across the Lifecourse: A Brief Introduction.* Basingstoke: Palgrave Macmillan.

Koomar, J., Kranowitz, C., Szklut, S., Balzer-Martin, L., Haber, E. and Sava, D.I. (2001) *Answers to Questions Teachers Ask about Sensory Integration: Forms, Checklists, and Practical Tools for Teachers and Parents.* Arlington, TX: Future Horizons.

Koren-Karie, N., Oppenheim, D., Dolev, S. and Yirmiya, N. (2009) 'Mothers of securely attached children with autism spectrum disorders are more sensitive than mothers of insecurely attached children.' *Journal of Child Psychology and Psychiatry 50,* 5, 643–650.

Kranowitz, C.S. (2005) *The Out-of-Sync Child: Recognizing and Coping with Sensory Processing Disorder.* New York: Perigree, revised edn (original work published 1998).

Main, M. and Solomon, J. (1986) 'Discovery of a New, Insecure Disorganized/Disorientated Attachment Pattern.' In T.B. Brazelton and M. Yogman (eds) *Affective Development in Infancy.* Norwood, NJ: Ablex.

Nash, J.M. (1997) 'How a child's brain develops.' *Time Magazine,* 3 February.

O'Driscoll, D. (2009) 'Psychotherapy and Intellectual Disability: A Historical View.' In T. Cottis (ed.) *Intellectual Disability, Trauma and Psychotherapy.* London: Routledge.

Panksepp, J. (2007) 'Can PLAY diminish ADHD and facilitate the construction of the social brain?' *Journal of Canadian Academic Child and Adolescent Psychiatry 16,* 2, 57–66.

Pianta, R.C. (2006) 'Teacher–Child Relationships and Early Literacy.' In D.K. Dickinson and S.B. Neuman (eds) *Handbook of Early Literacy Research, Volume 2.* New York: Guilford.

Rutter, M., Beckett, C., Castle, J., Kreppner, J., Stevens, S. and Sonuga-Barke, E. (2009) *Policy and Practice Implications from the English and Romanian Adoptees (ERA) Study: Forty-Five Key Questions.* London: BAAF.

Van IJzendoorn, M.H. and Sagi, A. (1999) 'Cross-Cultural Patterns of Attachment: Universal and Contextual Dimensions.' In J. Cassidy and P.R. Shaver (eds) *Handbook of Attachment: Theory, Research and Clinical Applications.* New York: Guilford.

Further Reading and Useful Websites

Further reading
Attachment theory

Bowlby, J. (1988/1998) *A Secure Base: Clinical Applications of Attachment Theory.* London: Routledge.

Cairns, K. (2002) *Attachment, Trauma and Resilience.* London: BAAF (British Association for Adopting and Fostering).

Howe, D. (2005) *Child Abuse and Neglect: Attachment, Development and Intervention.* Basingstoke: Palgrave Macmillan.

Howe, D. (2011) *Attachment across the Lifecourse: A Brief Introduction.* Basingstoke: Palgrave Macmillan.

Supporting children in early years settings and schools

Bebbington, E. (2012) *Stop Wasting my Time! Case Studies of Pupils with Attachment Issues in Schools with Special Reference to Looked After and Adopted Children.* Available at www.postadoptioncentralsupport.org (accessed 27 July 2012).

Bombèr, L.M. (2007) *Inside I'm Hurting: Practical Strategies for Supporting Children with Attachment Difficulties in School.* London: Worth.

Bombèr, L.M. (2011) *What about Me? Inclusive Strategies to Support Pupils with Attachment Difficulties Make It through the School Day.* London: Worth.

Cairns, K. and Stanway, C. (2004) *Learn the Child: Helping Looked After Children to Learn.* London: BAAF.

Elfer, P., Goldschmeid, E. and Selleck, D. (2002) *Key Persons in the Nursery: Building Relationships for Quality Provision.* London: Early Years Network.

Geddes, H. (2006) *Attachment in the Classroom: The Links Between Children's Early Experience, Emotional Well-Being and Performance in School.* London: Worth.

Mosley, J., Sonnet, H. and Barnes R. (2003) *101 Games for Social Skills.* Hyde, UK: LDA.

Read, V. (2010) *Developing Attachment in Early Years Settings: Nurturing Secure Relationships from Birth to Five Years.* London: Routledge.

Smith, C.A. (1998) *The Peaceful Classroom: Compassion and Cooperation Activities for Three- to Five-Year-Olds.* Edinburgh: Floris Books.

Children in care and adopted

Gilligan, R. (2001) *Promoting Resilience: A Resource Guide on Working with Children in the Care System.* London: BAAF.

Golding, K.S. (2006) *Thinking Psychologically about Children Who are Looked After and Adopted: Space for Reflection.* Chichester: Wiley.

Golding, K.S. (2008) *Nurturing Attachments: Supporting Children Who are Fostered or Adopted.* London: Jessica Kingsley Publishers.

Hughes, D.A. (2006) *Building the Bonds of Attachment: Awakening Love in Deeply Troubled Children,* 2nd edn. Lanham, MD: Aronson.

Parenting

Bailey, B. (2000) *I Love You Rituals.* New York: HarperCollins.

Cohen, L.J. (2001) *Playful Parenting.* New York: Ballantine.

Golding, K.S. and Hughes, D.A. (2012) *Creating Loving Attachments: Parenting with PACE to Nurture Confidence and Security in the Troubled Child.* London: Jessica Kingsley Publishers.

Hughes, D.A. (2009) *Attachment Focused Parenting: Effective Strategies to Care for Children.* New York: Norton.

Hughes, D.A. and Baylin, J. (2012) *Brain-Based Parenting. The Neuroscience of Caregiving for Healthy Attachment.* New York: Norton.

Sunderland, M. (2006) *The Science of Parenting: Practical Guidance on Sleep, Crying, Play and Building Emotional Well-Being for Life.* London: Dorling Kindersley.

Useful websites

All websites were accessed on 27 July 2012.

Help in educational settings

Nurture Group Network

The Nurture Group Network provides advice, support and information to support its aims of raising the profile of nurture and enabling access to nurture provision.
www.nurturegroups.org

Post Adoption Central Support (PACS)

Post Adoption Central Support has developed a leaflet about adoption and related attachment issues.
www.postadoptioncentralsupport.org

Protective Behaviours UK

Protective Behaviours UK provides information and resources related to protective behaviours approaches.
www.protectivebehaviours.co.uk

Yellow Kite
Attachment support service for schools. Yellow Kite offers a range of services supporting children in care and adopted children.
www.theyellowkite.co.uk

Young Minds in Schools
Young Minds in Schools supports the emotional well-being of children and young people in school. It aims to support educational professionals' understanding of the link between emotional well-being and learning.
http://youngmindsinschools.org.uk

Young Minds in Schools (Attachment, behaviour and learning)
This part of the website has a section covering the links between attachment, behaviour and learning and offering strategies for schools to support attachment.
www.youngminds.org.uk/training_services/young_minds_in_schools/wellbeing/attachment

Helping children with neurodevelopmental difficulties

ADHD Pages
This site provides an introduction to the ADHD Pages available on the Hi2u 4 people with hidden impairments website. A site centred around ADHD, Asperger syndrome, dyslexia and similar neurological differences along with any other type of hidden impairment.
www.adhd.org.uk

Brain Gym®
The Brain Gym® model of learning promotes play and the joy of learning while building awareness of the value of movement in daily life. It encourages creativity and self-expression and inspires an appreciation of music, physical education and the fine arts.
http://braingym.org.uk

Global Autism Collaboration
The Global Autism Collaboration is an organization created in response to a global need for networking and communication among autism groups.
http://autism.org

Gray Center
The Gray Center is the official home of Carol Gray and Social Stories™. This site provides samples and instructions for creating and using this educational tool to promote social understanding and social effectiveness.
www.thegraycenter.org

SenseToys
SenseToys provides a range of toys adapted for children with learning difficulties.
http://sensetoys.com

Sensory Direct

Sensory Direct designs, manufactures and distributes a range of weighted therapy products for children and adults.

http://sensorydirect.com

Sensory Integration Network

The Sensory Integration Network promotes education, good practice and research into the theory and practice of sensory integration.

www.sensoryintegration.org.uk

Theraplay® Institute

The Theraplay® Institute is an international organization with headquarters in Chicago, USA. The website provides information, resources and details of training in Theraplay®.

http://theraplay.org

Author Biographies

Kim S. Golding Kim is a consultant clinical psychologist with a special interest in supporting foster carers and adoptive parents. Kim was involved in the setting up and evaluation of an inter-agency project in Worcestershire. This team is now part of the Integrated Service for Looked After and Adopted Children (ISL). The team provides support for foster, adoptive and residential carers, schools and the range of professionals around the child growing up in care. Within this service Kim has developed a range of direct and indirect interventions based on attachment theory, and has carried out research exploring the use of a consultation service for foster carers and other professionals. Kim has a passionate interest in getting the emotional needs of children better understood within schools and early years settings. She is concerned that too much focus on behavioural management and a focus on learning without strengthening emotional and social development means that some children are not able to get the best out of their time in school, with continuing difficulties in forming healthy relationships.

Jane Fain After many years caring for her four children as a full-time mum, Jane began working in nurseries and preschool. As her youngest child started nursery, she became interested in working in this sector and began working in a nursery. She completed a level 3 BTEC in Childhood Studies while running a local preschool group. She then went on to work as a teaching assistant in a local school. Jane joined ISL in 2002 as an early years practitioner supporting the transition of children from their early years education setting into school. Jane reflects: 'While working for the team I became aware of attachment difficulties, something I had not heard of before. This made me consider and reflect on the children I was supporting and how their early life experiences would shape their view of the world. It also helped me to consider what might lie behind some of the challenging behaviours being described to me by fellow early years practitioners who were concerned by behaviours some children were displaying and requested strategies for supporting these children. I was keen to share the knowledge I had gained and I felt as a service we needed something that would help ISL to share our knowledge of attachment with early educators.'

Ann Frost Ann has worked for ISL since 2008. She works within early years and education, supporting looked after and adopted children by raising awareness of their additional needs in schools and early years settings. Ann trained and worked within the early years for a number of years, before taking a break to complete a degree in psychology and then to stay at home while her two children were young. She returned to work gradually by first supporting a child with additional needs in school and then working within the early years in a local education authority setting before gaining employment within ISL. Ann reflects: 'I often hear myself saying if I knew then (in my previous posts), what I know now, then my practice would have been very different. I still have children's faces etched in my memory who may have benefited from this approach.'

Cathy Mills Cathy started teaching in 1977 in Dudley West Midlands as a full-time teacher in a primary school; a strength with special needs children was recognized by the headteacher, who helped her to develop this skill. After the birth of her children, she joined Hereford and Worcester Special Educational Needs Services to schools and worked throughout the area. After a number of years she returned to teaching within a school as a full-time class teacher and SENCO with a high proportion of pupils with special needs. After approximately ten years and having experienced the needs of looked after children within her class, she joined ISL as a support teacher to schools. In 2011 she retired as a teacher for the service but continues to be involved working on a sessional basis with the Greenfingers project, which offers therapeutic gardening and art sessions to looked after children and their carers within Worcestershire.

Helen Worrall Prior to working as a support teacher in ISL, Helen was a primary school teacher, working in schools in Wolverhampton and Walsall between 1995 and 2004. She soon found that she had a particular passion and skill for working with children who had special needs – especially those who had a variety of emotional needs which impacted upon their learning. In 2004 she took up a post for ISL and began working to support looked after and adopted children to enjoy and achieve in education.

Netty Roberts Netty came into teaching via a career in hairdressing and retail businesses. When her children were young, as a hobby, she revisited sign language roots following her early experiences with her deaf grandmother. She decided to take this to the next level and began communicating and supporting hearing impaired students in high school and further education college. She decided to retrain and achieved Qualified Teacher Status in primary education. After teaching in middle school, her interest in special needs took her to an able autistic unit attached to a mainstream middle school. She then took the role of Foundation and Key Stage 1 teacher within ISL in 2008. She reflects: 'As part of my new role I had to learn about disrupted attachments and the impact on brain development in relation to learning. I was appalled that I hadn't been made aware of this while I was working in the classroom. Indeed, why wasn't I taught this at university? As I sat on my first attachment course, I sat there mentally naming children that I had taught in the past and some of their behaviours made sense – finally.'

Eleanor Durrant Eleanor graduated with a psychology degree in 2005. She spent several years working as a behaviour analyst with children with developmental disorders and learning disabilities. This work took place both in and out of the classroom and highlighted to her the barriers some children have in accessing the curriculum. As an assistant psychologist within the Child and Adolescent Mental Health Services (CAMHS), Family Intervention Project (FIP) and ISL, she enjoyed working therapeutically with looked after children and others with attachment difficulties. Currently in her first year of a clinical psychology doctorate, attachment continues to be a strong area of interest and she intends to complete her third year research in this field.

Sian Templeton Sian has worked as an educational psychologist in Worcestershire since 2000. Her initial psychology training was at Cardiff University, graduating in 1993. She then went on to complete a postgraduate certificate of education at Swansea University before teaching for four years in primary education. In 1999 she completed a masters degree in educational psychology at Exeter University, gaining a distinction.